Let Us Enjoy Forgiveness

Judson Cornwall

1 John 1:9

BY Judson Cornwall

Let Us Abide
Let Us Enjoy Forgiveness

Let Us
Enjoy
Forgiveness

Judson Cornwall

Fleming H. Revell Company
Old Tappan, New Jersey

Library of Congress Cataloging in Publication Data

Cornwall, Judson.
   Let us enjoy forgiveness.

   1. Forgiveness of sin. I. Title.
BT795.C67   234'.5   78-8306
ISBN 0-8007-0945-4

Contents

Preface   11

1 **The Promise of Forgiveness**   15
God wants us to learn to enjoy forgiveness and to
enjoy living as forgiven people.

2 **The Perversity Requiring Forgiveness**   27
Sin has indeed broken our contact with the Di-
vine, has desensitized us to things spiritual, and
consequently has so imbalanced us as to break
our fellowship with others.

3 **The Purchase of Forgiveness**   43
"It is finished," He cried and at that moment
every price that God would ever extract for sin,
every penalty that could ever be levied for violation of God's law, and every cent that was owed
because of sin was paid in full.

4 **The Preparation for Forgiveness**   53
Repentance unlocks the door of our life, thereby
enabling us to receive divine mercy and grace.

5 **The Phraseology of Forgiveness**   73
If there is one central theme to be seen in reading
the many Scriptures that contain the word *forgive,* it is that God wants to forgive.

6 **The Process of Forgiveness**   85
God's forgiveness ransoms his man, pays his
debts, and restores him to sonship.

7 **The Proportion of Forgiveness**   103
   When we focus our attention on God's side of
   forgiveness, we are assured that there will never
   be condemnation at this time handed down
   against any person who has sincerely and scripturally repented.

8 **The Pattern of Forgiveness**   125
   So great is God's forgiveness that He not only
   removes the penalty for past sin but has provided
   a preventive to future involvement in sin.

9 **The Purpose of Forgiveness**   137
   The highest purpose of forgiveness is to allow
   God to manifest His lovingkindness and tender
   mercies and thereby declare, demonstrate, and
   dispense His glory among men.

10 **The Perpetuity of Forgiveness**   147
   Let's stop listening to our memory circuits and
   reprogram our minds to enjoy our new status as
   forgiven and loved people.

Acknowledgments

Behind every major project are the unseen and unsung workers who contribute expertise and advise. Notable among them on this undertaking is Cheryl Tipon, my secretary, who invested many hours in manuscript corrections and suggestions for better ways of expression. Thanks.

And, as always, my wife has again sacrificed hundreds of hours of companionship so I could write this book. This time she even went to Argentina to spend the Christmas holidays with our daughters, leaving me at home undisturbed and unhindered for writing. Those who read this book may not understand what this cost her, but God keeps the records and will reward accordingly.

Preface

In the summer of 1977 I was one of the speakers at a camp meeting amid the beautiful redwoods near Santa Cruz, California. The food was served outdoors, cafeteria style, and my wife and I had been instructed to go directly to the head of the line and cut in. At the first meal that I apologetically took someone else's place, I was greeted with, "Oh, thank God it's you, Brother Cornwall. I was wondering how I would ever get a chance to talk to you. You see, this morning while you were preaching I felt that the Lord would be very pleased if you would write a book on forgiveness."

Taking paper and pen out of my pocket, I made a very obvious display of writing it down and then went on with my meal, but when I got to my room the Lord reproved me for mocking a suggestion that had really come from Him. I repented, and then took a serious look at what the Lord wanted.

Two nights later the Lord gave me the entire outline for this book, chapter by chapter, and when Fleming H. Revell Company read this outline, they contracted to publish the book as soon as it could be written. I was on my way.

In my research I found very little literature dealing with God's forgiveness, for most of the current material is concerned with man forgiving man. Many of the commentaries and encyclopedias declare that man's forgiveness and God's forgiveness can be equated; and then spend the space talking about man's forgiveness.

But I am convinced that man's forgiveness will never equal God's forgiveness, for ours is a low-level substitute; a reflection in a poor-quality mirror. Because we have too often thought of God's forgiveness as being the same as ours, few of us have come to really enjoy divine forgiveness. We do not know how vast and valuable it really is.

This book deals almost exclusively with God's forgiveness of man, and its intent is to make each of us aware of how completely He has released us from every facet of sin. This is why we say, *Let Us Enjoy Forgiveness*.

Let Us Enjoy Forgiveness

1

The Promise of Forgiveness

"Popular T.V. Star Shoots Self."

"Heroin Use Soars in U.S."

"Two Tons of Nerve Pills Consumed Daily in States."

"One in Three Marriages in America Ends in Divorce."

"Heart Attack Still Number-One Killer of Males."

Pulp-magazine teasers? No! Just headlines common to our daily newspapers. Tension is rampant, and coping with it has a high priority in almost everyone's life. Those who don't learn to adjust to it usually collapse physically, break down emotionally, withdraw from reality, or self-destruct one way or another.

Can the full blame for these tensions be placed on the fast pace of our American culture? Some sociologists seem to think so and often project withdrawal to serenity as the ultimate answer to tension. Suburbia or the lakeside cabin are classic examples.

Still, King David, many thousands of years ago, wrote of his tension, depression, and heart trouble; yet who could live in a more placid environment than he did? David did not blame the pace of life for his inner conflicts. He blamed guilt. His poetic way of describing his condition is recorded in Psalms 32, which is a companion song to Psalms 51; both of which were written shortly after the prophet Nathan brought God's word of judgment upon David for his adultery with Bathsheba and the subsequent murder of her husband to cover up the act. How graphically and accurately David describes the very physical responses, emotional trauma, and the mental depression that drive millions of people in this generation to seek chemical relief.

In verse 3 he describes his physical reactions to the load of guilt: "When I declared not my sin, my body wasted away through my groaning all day long" (Psalms 32:3 RSV). David seemed to be physically exhausted continuously, although there was no activity to produce such tiredness. Not only was he fatigued; he was frustrated. The Living Bible translates this verse: "There was a time when I wouldn't admit what a sinner I was. But my dishonesty made me miserable and filled my days with frustration." It sounds familiar, doesn't it? Fatigue and frustration, all due to inner pressures, with no letup. In the next verse David cried, "All day and all night your hand was heavy on me . . ." (Psalms 32:4 LB). The final phrase of this verse has been translated from the Aramaic by George Lamsa in *The Holy Bible From Ancient Eastern Manuscripts* as: "Intense pain developed in my heart great enough to kill me." First fatigue, next frustration, and now heart failure, and all because of unremitted guilt.

Thousands of American doctors and psychiatrists hear these symptoms daily. The pain is genuine, and the mental disturbance is alarming, but often the doctors are baffled in trying to pinpoint the cause.

David didn't have any trouble accepting the divine diagnosis. He admitted that he was guilty of sin and that God's threatened punishment was consuming him.

By verse 5 David had suffered long enough. He cried: ". . . I will confess my transgressions unto the Lord . . . ." How humbling this must have been for Israel's most popular king. But the pressure that guilt produces became unbearable, even for an absolute monarch. He ceased pleading his merit and began to plead for God's mercy: "Have mercy upon me, O God, according to thy lovingkindness: according unto the multitude of thy tender mercies . . ." (Psalms 51:1). His guilt and its effects had gone beyond anything that he, his counselors, his physicians, his army, or his wealth could handle. If God didn't help him, he was headed for a nervous breakdown or a heart failure. Under these circumstances, humbling himself to confess his sin seemed safer than continuing to resist God.

Immediately after David said, ". . . I will confess them to the Lord," he exclaimed, "And you forgave me! All my guilt is gone" (Psalms 32:5 LB). Instant response—immediate relief—intense rejoicing. When he stopped treating the symptoms and tried confessing the cause, God corrected both the cause and the symptoms.

David's joy is expressed in the introductory verses of this psalm: "What happiness for those whose guilt has been forgiven! What joys when sins are covered over! What relief for those who have confessed their sins and God has cleared their record" (Psalms 32:1, 2 LB).

Has humanity changed since the days of David? Has the keen expansion of man's mind developed an immunity to the powerful workings of guilt in his nature? I think not. The statistics on nervous breakdowns, heart failures, drug abuse, alcoholism, sexual perversion, and amusement (*a* is a prefix meaning "not" and *muse* means "to think"—hence amusement is that which prevents us from thinking) seem to prove exactly the opposite. For although man may seek to

change the standards and mores whereby guilt is deter-
mined, God has concluded all men to be guilty: "For all
have sinned, and come short of the glory of God" (Romans
3:23). Almost irrespective of the imputation of man's intellect, guilt will eventually surface in his heart and become a
destructive energy throughout his entire system, for
". . . sin, when it is finished, bringeth forth death" (James
1:15).

But while this cause-effect of sin and guilt may be irrevocable, it is not irreversible. Although no one can "un-
sin" he can confess sin and be absolved of the guilt of that
sin, cleansed from the stain of that sin, and delivered from
the power of it. In scriptural terms he is justified, sanctified,
and glorified. Christ Jesus bears the penalty of the guilt, the
Holy Spirit applies the cleansing from the guilt, while God
the Father shares the glory of our guiltless relationship with
Him as His children and heirs.

That this is the only way the sinner can find peace with
God is well accepted in most religious circles, however varied their application may be. But please recognize that
David was not a sinner in the most popular sense of that
word. He was already a saint in the New Testament sense
of the word. He had been chosen of God and commissioned
to be king over all Israel long before this incident. He had
known long dealings of God through the insane jealousy of
Saul, and had slowly fulfilled the will of God in uniting the
twelve tribes into one nation. His faithful warring against
Israel's enemies had greatly enlarged her territory and had
brought her security. He had brought the ark back to
Jerusalem and had established the Tabernacle of David
spoken of by the prophets and in the New Testament (*see*
Amos 9:11; Acts 15:16).

Besides this, David was a worshiper and had taught
others to worship God with instruments, with vocal singing,

and in the dance. By the standards of today's church, he was preeminently successful. He had achieved most of his goals; he had fulfilled God's calling; he was respected by his brethren, followed by his people, and beloved by his God. Still, he sinned a grievous sin, thereby heaping upon himself such a load of guilt that at one point he despaired of being able to live through it.

The wages of sin are the same for the sinner and the saint. Unconfessed sin loads any man with guilt, regardless of past encounters with God and His grace. As surely as it is not a man's prior confession of fault but his present participation in sin that lights the fire of shame and remorse within him, so the previous forgiveness God may have granted does not carry through to cover transgressions after that pardon. Sin must be dealt with as it occurs. While forgiveness may be retroactive, it can never be postdated. Confession must be contemporary if forgiveness is to be current.

This is why the Bible speaks of Christians, not sinners, confessing their sins. Sinners are merely asked to confess Christ Jesus as Lord (*see* Romans 10:9, 10). It is the reason that forgiveness, pardon, cleansing, justification, and deliverance are consistently offered to the Christian and are discussed in context with great doctrinal provisions that have always been accepted as the exclusive right of Christians. To the *saints,* it is written: "If *we* say that *we* have no sin, *we* deceive ourselves, and the truth is not in *us*. If *we* confess *our* sins, he is faithful and just to forgive *us our* sins, and to cleanse *us* from all unrighteousness" (1 John 1:8, 9, emphasis added). Since nothing else in John's epistle is directed to sinners, surely this cannot be a message to them hidden in a letter to the saints.

Sin affects the believer's will, his walk, and his witness. It endangers his life, weakens his love, and restricts his liberty. It is sin that separates the Christian from fellowship with his Lord (*see* Isaiah 59:2). It is sin that causes prayers to go unanswered (*see* Psalms 66:18). It is sin that brings divine chastisement upon the believer (*see* 2 Samuel 7:14), and ultimately sin brings death, both natural and spiritual (*see* Jeremiah 31:30; Romans 6:23).

God's Forgiving Nature

But as serious as sin is, it is no problem for God. He negated the sin question once and forever in the death of Jesus Christ on Calvary's cross. Sin may consistently be a problem for the saint and insistently an enigma for the church, but it is indefectibly settled as far as God is concerned. God's laws were answered in Christ's death, His saints were cleansed by Christ's blood, and the power of sin was broken in Christ's resurrection. God need do nothing more. "It is finished" (*see* John 19:30).

But God did not settle the sin question to His satisfaction and then leave man to struggle under the weight of sin's guilt. He promised to freely and fully forgive sinful man, thereby remitting all guilt to Calvary. To rebellious Israel, chafing under God's chastisement as vassal slaves to Babylon, God declared, "In those days, and in that time, saith the Lord, the iniquity of Israel shall be sought for, and there shall be none; and the sins of Judah, and they shall not be found: *for I will pardon them* whom I reserve" (Jeremiah 50:20, emphasis added). They were chastened and then cleansed; sent into captivity to produce confession and then pardoned to perfection, so that no sins could be found.

This promise of forgiveness was covenanted to Moses when the Lord passed by him as he stood in the cleft of the rock. Since God cannot swear by anything greater than Himself (*see* Hebrews 6:13), He proclaimed His name to Moses, declaring, ". . . The Lord God, merciful and gracious, longsuffering, and abundant in goodness and truth,

Keeping mercy for thousands, *forgiving iniquity* and *transgression* and *sin . . .''* (Exodus 34:6, 7, emphasis added). Forgiveness is part of the declared nature of God. He does not have to be in the mood to forgive; it is in His nature to forgive. We are not required to earn His forgiveness, but merely to ask for it, for He is far more anxious to forgive us our sin than we are to forsake our sin.

Moses grasped the import of this covenant, for when the negative report of the ten spies stirred a revolt in Israel, inciting refusal to go into the land of God's promise, God told Moses to stand aside while He destroyed them all. In his intercession Moses reminded God of His very nature and of His covenant pledge and cried, "Pardon, I beseech thee, the iniquity of this people according unto the greatness of thy mercy, and as thou hast forgiven this people, from Egypt even until now. And the Lord said, I have pardoned according to thy word'' (Numbers 14:19, 20). The sin was grievous, the rebellion rampant, and God's anger was furious. But when a plea for forgiveness was entered, God could not violate His essential nature. He is a forgiving God. Hallelujah!

The historic books of the Old Testament abound with understanding of God's forgiveness. Consider God's continued forgiveness during the times of the judges; or the beautiful type of redemption in the book of Ruth; or when Israel sinned in demanding a king and God terrorized her with physical demonstrations following which "Samuel said unto the people, Fear not: ye have done all this wickedness: yet turn not aside from following the Lord . . . For the Lord will not forsake his people for his great name's sake: because it hath pleased the Lord to make you his people'' (1 Samuel 12:20, 22). Even their rejection of God's leadership did not prove to be beyond God's forgiveness.

The psalmists also understood this forgiving nature of

God. They wrote: "But he, being full of compassion, forgave . . ." (Psalms 78:38); "Thou hast forgiven the iniquity of thy people, thou hast covered all their sin . . ." (Psalms 85:2); ". . . thou wast a God that forgavest them . . ." (Psalms 99:8); "Who forgiveth all thine iniquities . . ." (Psalms 103:3); and "If thou, Lord, shouldest mark iniquities, O Lord, who shall stand? But there is forgiveness with thee . . . for with the Lord there is mercy, and with him is plenteous redemption" (Psalms 130:3, 4, 7). Much of the occasion for the writing of a psalm was the response to forgiveness of sin. The lifting of the load of guilt brought a lilting to their lives which could best be expressed in a song and a dance before the Lord.

The prophets, too, were given insight into this forgiving nature of God. Isaiah declared, "He will abundantly pardon" (*see* Isaiah 55:7). Jeremiah wrote, ". . . and I will pardon all their iniquities . . . I will pardon them whom I reserve" (Jeremiah 33:8; 50:20). Hosea, after calling for Israel to return unto the Lord, prophesied, "I will heal their backsliding, I will love them freely: for mine anger is turned away from him" (Hosea 14:4). The life of Jonah and God's forgiveness of Nineveh profusely illustrate how far-reaching God's forgiveness really is—so far that it inspired Zephaniah to write, "The Lord thy God in the midst of thee is mighty; *he will save,* he will rejoice over thee with joy; he will rest in his love, he will joy over thee with singing" (Zephaniah 3:17, emphasis added).

Because He Himself was God, Jesus understood the forgiving nature of the Father and proclaimed it widely in the Gospels, from including it in the model prayer: "Forgive us our debts . . . your heavenly Father will also forgive you . . ." (Matthew 6:12, 14), to demanding it from his disciples (*see* Matthew 18:21, 22), and horrifying the religious society by openly forgiving sin and repeatedly telling offenders that He did not condemn them (*see* Matthew 9:2–6; John 8:11). Even in death Christ forgave the repentant thief hanging on a cross. What God promised and proclaimed, Christ plied and paraded. While the declaration may be misunderstood, the demonstration is unmistakable—God forgives confessed sin.

The New Testament's one book of history, the Acts, gives us three separate accounts of Paul's conversion, so great was this demonstration of God's great forgiveness. Repentance is preached from Peter's message on the day of Pentecost through Paul's missionary journeys. At Philippi Paul told the jailer, ". . . Believe on the Lord Jesus Christ, and thou shalt be saved, and thy house" (Acts 16:31), and at Rome, in the last chapter of the book, Paul declared, "Be it known therefore unto you, that the salvation of God is sent unto the Gentiles, and that they will hear it" (Acts 28:28). The early church's missionary program was predicated on God's forgiveness.

The Pauline epistles delve doctrinally into the magnanimous mercy of God's forgiveness. Paul declares: "There is therefore now no condemnation to them which are in Christ Jesus . . ." (Romans 8:1); ". . . God for Christ's sake hath forgiven you (Ephesians 4:32); "In whom we have redemption through his blood, even the forgiveness of sins" (Colossians 1:14). Paul wrote experientially about forgiveness, for the misdirected zeal that made him a slaughterer of Christians was pardoned and he subsequently lived the life of a forgiven man. So great was his appreciation for this forgiveness that he called himself a slave of the Lord Jesus Christ.

Similarly, the general epistles are just as aware of God's forgiving nature as Moses was. Hebrews declares, "For by one offering he [Jesus] hath perfected for ever them that are sanctified" (Hebrews 10:14). James 5:15 says, ". . . and if he have committed sins, they shall be forgiven him." Peter writes, "Forasmuch as ye know that ye were not redeemed with corruptible things, as silver and gold . . . But with the precious blood of Christ . . ." (1 Peter 1:18, 19), while John encourages the believers with, "I write unto you . . . because your sins are forgiven you for his name's sake" (1 John 2:12). In concluding the epistles, Jude breaks forth into the beautiful doxology: "Now unto him that is able to keep you from falling, and to present you faultless before the presence of his glory with exceeding joy . . ." (Jude 24).

Can anyone read the prophetic book of the New Testament without gaining an awareness that it is a book of the consummation of redemption? ". . . Unto him that loved us, and washed us from our sins in his own blood . . ." (Revelation 1:5); ". . . Thou . . . hast redeemed us to God by thy blood out of every kindred, and tongue, and people, and nation" (Revelation 5:9); "And they overcame him by the blood of the Lamb . . ." (Revelation 12:11); ". . . I heard a great voice of much people in heaven, saying, Alleluia; Salvation, and glory, and honour, and power, unto the Lord our God" (Revelation 19:1); "And I heard a great voice out of heaven saying, Behold, the tabernacle of God is with men, and he will dwell with them, and they shall be his people, and God himself shall be with them, and be their God. And God shall wipe away all tears from their eyes; and there shall be no more death, neither sorrow, nor crying, neither shall there be any more pain: for the former things are passed away" (Revelation 21:3, 4). This is forgiveness in full perfection; salvation in its completed state.

There is no mistaking it—God offers forgiveness. All any man must do is repent and forsake his sin, and God will forgive him and will revoke the penalty of sin, because God has consistently promised forgiveness of sin. This forgiveness is a promise of the Father, a provision of the Son, a proclamation in the Word, and a required practice in the church. Man is urged to flee not from but to the triune God and his church when the sin question becomes burdensome. God's provision is man's only deliverance from the pangs of guilt. God wants us to learn to enjoy forgiveness and to enjoy living as forgiven people.

2

The Perversity Requiring Forgiveness

"Pardon me," "excuse me," "I'm terribly sorry," are polite expressions we hear daily. They indicate that some discourtesy has been done but suggest that it was not intentional. Usually forgiveness is automatically given, but occasionally someone will express an unforgiving attitude which is met with a "but I said I'm sorry."

Words cannot be recalled nor deeds undone. Having said the unkind thing, you cannot unsay it, although we may awkwardly try to cover it over with another statement. Having stepped on a person's foot in a crowded elevator, there is no way to unstep on it. Restoration is impossible. Only forgiveness can be sought. If it is denied, both the offender and the offended suffer—the one with guilt and the other with resentment. A minor offense becomes a major issue when forgiveness is denied.

Behind every polite "excuse me" is obviously a rule of etiquette that has been broken, for if there were no law, no rule, no code of ethics, there would never have been an offense. But society as we know it could not continue to exist without rules and laws that govern our behavior. Driving would be a disaster without traffic laws to give uniformity to behavior, and business transactions would be utterly impossible if every man did that which was right in his own eyes.

Obviously, then, for these laws to be effective there must be built-in penalties for the lawbreaker, for without penalty the law is little more than a suggestion and is totally unenforceable.

Surely God, the great lawgiver, had this in mind when He warned, "The soul that sinneth, it shall die . . ." (Ezekiel 18:20). This built-in penalty for breaking God's law is far more severe than the recently revived penalty of the Koran in Moslem countries, which provides for the severing of the hand of a thief or public flogging for lesser offenses. Although these offenders may be maimed for life, at least they survived the penalty of the law, but none can survive the penalties built into God's law, "The one who sins is the one who dies . . ." (Ezekiel 18:20 LB).

Why is God so extremely severe in dealing with sin? Simply because sin is a broken law, a broken relationship, a broken fellowship, and it produces a broken life. Without God's intervention, sin will produce its own death. Unless pardon is received, sinful man will be destroyed by his own guilt. No man has yet lived who did not need the forgiveness of God, for Romans 3:23 affirms: "For all have sinned, and come short of the glory of God." In one way or another we have all violated God's law and need His forgiveness.

Consider, first of all, how universally we need forgiveness for breaking God's law. First John 3:4 informs us, ". . . sin is the transgression of the law." Of course, ". . . where no law is, there is no transgression" (Romans 4:15), but this cannot apply to this generation of enlightened people, for we have the Bible available to us in a great variety of translations, and we have churches, books, cassettes, Christian radio and TV to regularly expound these laws of God to us. Certainly we "are without excuse" (*see* Romans 1:20). But even where these are unavailable, God's law holds valid, for ignorance of the law cannot invalidate it. The law works whether we understand it or not; yet our knowledge of the law makes it possible for us to cooperate with that law and benefit from it. But knowledge of the law and obedience to that law are two separate actions. "Therefore to him that knoweth to do good, and doeth it not, to him it is sin" (James 4:17).

We must constantly bear in mind that the purpose of law is not to ruin but to regulate. God has not capriciously codified commandments to destroy man or even to inhibit the expression of his created nature. Man is the zenith of God's creation and the object of His love. God's intent in giving us law is to restore us to harmonious relationships with ourselves, with others, and with Himself. His law is similar to a manufacturer's book of instructions, showing how a product can best be used. Violate the instructions and the product may not work at all or may have a greatly shortened life span.

So God's law has been given to direct us in the proper use of our bodies, minds, souls, and spirits and to make viable relationships both possible and meaningful. Lawlessness, a condition of being without law, can bring only ruin. But so will insubordination, rebellion, and anarchy, which are refusals to submit to the law. For all of the examples human history has afforded us showing that rebellion to divine laws always brings ruin, there is something within each of us that prefers to do things our own way. This forms the true hub of sin. Isaiah 53:6 quite accurately states, ". . . we have turned every one to his own way; and the Lord hath laid on him the iniquity of us all." It is this turning to our own way that became the iniquity which sent Christ to Calvary. It is wanting my own way versus submitting to God's revealed way that introduces sin into my life. Long before that sin matures into evil deeds, my life becomes iniquitous because of evil desires—my own way.

So the perversity requiring forgiveness is, in its most elementary form, the exercise of self-will against the known will of God. But obviously this is an oversimplification, for sin is far more insidious, far more complex, far more deceitful than mere rebellion. The inworking of sin affects the whole nature of man, and the outworking of sin violates the complete character of God. In trying to help us understand the complexity of sin, the Bible uses at least twelve different words in the original languages, each one giving a different shade of understanding. So great is this thing called sin that no one word can amply define it.

The Many Shades of Sin

Look, first of all, at the wealth of Hebrew words used in the Old Testament to define and explain sin and iniquity. Noticeable among them is the word *aven,* which is translated "wickedness" in a few places and "iniquity" in thirty-eight places. Many students of the Hebrew language declare that the original meaning of this word is "nothingness." It is used in connection with idolatry on repeated occasions, signifying that an idol is a nothing, a vain thing. In Hosea 4:15 and 5:8 Bethel, the House of God, is designated as Beth-*aven*, the house of vanity or nothingness, because idols were worshiped there.

In several passages this word is translated as "vanity" (*see* Job 15:35; Psalms 10:7; Proverbs 22:8 and others). The book of Ecclesiastes fully defines the scriptural meaning of vanity as "emptiness," "nothingness," "the wind," "a vapor," and so forth. It is that which lacks substance, meaning, or purpose. It is a mirage in the desert, a projected image on the screen, a shadow in the night. Such is the Bible definition of sin. Like Satan's lie to Eve in the garden, ". . . ye shall be as gods . . ." (Genesis 3:5), so sin promises us great things but gives us nothing. By using this word *aven,* the inspired writers put a stamp of unreality or empty nothingness upon every departure from the law of God, no matter what form that departure may take. All of man's evil devices are false, hollow, and unreal. Sin is a nothingness. Ask any converted addict.

A second Hebrew word used in the Old Testament which helps define sin is *ma'al* which, the scholars tell us, seems to point to the unfaithfulness and treachery of sin. It pictures sin as a breach of trust either between man and man or between man and his God. Thirty times this word is translated "trespass" and fifteen times it is rendered "transgression." In Job 21:34 it is forcibly called "falsehood."

Since the law of first reference is so important to Bible students, it is interesting that the first time this word occurs in the Bible (Leviticus 5:15) it refers to a trespass committed in ignorance, and in its second occurrence it is concerned with any sin committed against one's neighbor (Leviticus 6:2). It is the word used to describe Achan's sin (Joshua 7:11; 22:20) and is also applied to Uzziah (2 Chronicles 26:18); to Ahaz (2 Chronicles 28:22); to Manasseh (2 Chronicles 33:19); and to the people who married heathen wives (Ezra 9:2, 4; Nehemiah 13:27). Note that the people guilty of sin in this *ma'al* aspect were chiefly persons in authority. They had abused a trust that had been committed to them. Much had been given to them, and much was required of them.

When we reread Genesis 1 and 2 and see the tremendous trust and responsibility God commissioned to man, and then realize how treacherously we have dealt with this authority, we better understand why God likens us to an unfaithful wife. Our sin has become a *ma'al,* an unfaithful breach of trust. By Webster's definition of the word we could call ourselves wicked—"morally bad; causing or likely to cause harm or trouble." And the Scriptures frequently use this very word to describe perpetrators of sin, or the companion word *wickedness* to describe their actions.

When this is done, the Hebrew word *rasha'* is the most generally used word (nearly 300 times). Scholars tell us that originally the word referred to the activity, the tossing, and the confusion in which the wicked live, and the perpetual agitation which they cause others. Accordingly, Isaiah says, "But the wicked are like the troubled sea, when it cannot rest, whose waters cast up mire and dirt. There is no peace, saith my God, to the wicked" (Isaiah 57:20, 21).

We could get a positive affirmation to this from almost any counseling psychiatrist, police officer, or minister. Sin produces an inner turmoil that cannot be stopped any more than the waves of the sea can be forced to cease. Even though man may not know the source of his fermentation (and none do except by divine revelation) it continues to work like yeast in the dough. Look at the multiplied millions of dollars we Americans spend annually in our attempt to quiet this inner tempest. We use alcohol, drugs, spectator sports, amusement, and sex in our attempt to quiet the inner agitation. Yet when we leave the cocktail lounge, the game, the place of amusement, or whatever, we slowly realize that the inner waves are still ceaselessly pounding on the sands of our heart. Wickedness in any form produces turbulence.

But, unfortunately, this turbulence is not confined to the life of the wicked. *Rasha'* refers not only to ceaseless activity and tossing in which the wicked live, but equally to the agitation which they cause others. Witness the turmoil one wicked child can cause in a godly home. Or share the tempest of the hostages on a hijacked plane. The pounding surf of wickedness in others affects everyone within range. Godly men and women, through their taxes, have to support prison systems and all the police and judicial systems behind the prison. The wickedness of others creates a tornado that affects us all.

But as surely as jetties do not stop the ocean waves and early storm warnings do not stop the hurricane, all of our attempts to control, lessen, restrict, or stop the activity and restlessness which wickedness produces are in vain. Only by getting to the root cause of the trouble—sin—can the storm be calmed. It still takes Jesus to command, "Peace, be still." Man's true problem is neither his ghetto environment nor his affluent society; it is sin. "There is no peace, saith my God, to the wicked" (Isaiah 57:21), and, as the psalmist so often depicted, these wicked are busily occupied in disturbing the peace of others. How comforting to realize that after His resurrection Christ Jesus constantly greeted His disciples with the blessing, "Peace be unto you" (*see* John 20:21). Not only does forgiveness calm our personal storm; it affords a relationship with Christ that shelters us from the agitation others would try to cause in our lives.

Anyone reading the Old Testament in its original languages will come across the Hebrew word *ra'* over 550 times and in all but about 100 of these occurrences, the word has been translated "evil" in the King James Version. It is also rendered "calamity," "distress," "adversity," "grief," "affliction," "misery," "sorrow," "trouble," "noisome," "hurt," and "wretchedness," but reading the passages where these other renderings are given, we gain a sense that it implies injury done to a person but does not touch upon its moral aspect. *Ra'*, etymologists tell us, depicts breaking up or ruin. It is a word which couples together the wicked deed and its consequences. It unites cause and effect, the act and the reaction, but does not concern itself with the moral factor involved.

Actually, *ra'* usually indicates the rough exterior of wrongdoing, as a breach of harmony, and as a breaking up of what is good and desirable in man and in society. Throughout the Scripture lovingkindness is given as the prominent characteristic of the godly, but by contrast one of the most conspicuous features of the ungodly man is that his behavior is an injury both to himself and to everyone around him. Not only is he an agitation—*ma'al*—he is injurious—*ra'*. This word is also used in Nahum 2:1. "He that dasheth in pieces is come up before thy face . . . ." When we look at the homes that have been scattered by the evil of divorce, or the lives that have been dashed to pieces by the evil of murder; when we visualize the minds that have been shattered by drugs and the bodies that have been destroyed by the evil of smoking or the evil of venereal diseases, we recognize that "he that dasheth to pieces is come . . . ."

Sin, evil, *ra'* is the great destroyer. Most people prefer to blame the devil for destruction in human life, but the Scripture blames sin. Evil produces its own consequences. Wrongdoing breaks up what little good there may be in life, leaving us with little more than shattered dreams and tainted memories. Without divine forgiveness the consequences of *ra'* are irrevocable.

And, unfortunately, even after complete forgiveness many of the consequences of *ra'* will still be reaped, for coming to Christ does not of itself assure that broken marriages will be mended, that broken bodies will be healed, minds restored, or those we have murdered raised to life.

Divine forgiveness does not pay off deep financial obligations that *ra'* often produces nor heal the broken hearts of
friends and loved ones. How we need to remind ourselves
over and over again that sin is not only a violation of God's
law and will, but also a destructive force in our personal life
and in society as a whole. Sin vainly promises us a lie
(*'aven*) but gives us destruction (*ra'*). Like the pictures in
the seed catalog, it assures us of something good, but
". . . sin, when it is finished, bringeth forth death" (James
1:15).

Since sin is obviously so consequential and so adversely
affects the participant as well as the bystander, why do men
continue to sin? Cannot rational man recognize his course
of self-destruction and change his behavior or learn from
another's tragedy?

Intellectually he is capable, but morally he is not. Many a
doctor who advises his patients to stop smoking for health's
sake is himself a chain smoker. Officers who spend the night
rounding up drunks often stop by a bar on their way home.
This is not an aberration of our affluent society, but a curse
of human nature. Even in Paul's day this principle was at
work. He asks: ". . . thou that preachest a man should not
steal, dost thou steal? Thou that sayest a man should not
commit adultery, dost thou commit adultery? . . . (Romans
2:21, 22). While the mind can grasp the consequences of
sin, the soul of man is gripped by a principle which prevents
him from acting positively upon the information his mind is
giving him. That principle is another facet of sin—rebellion.

The Hebrew word *pasha'* is usually translated
"transgression" in the King James Bible, but it projects the
concept of revolting or refusing to be subject to rightful
authority. It is the word used in Job 34:37 where it is said of
him that "he addeth rebellion unto his sin . . . ." Isaiah
also used it in saying, ". . . I have nourished and brought

up children, and they have rebelled against me'' (Isaiah 1:2). Sin is a rebellion against authority, a rejection of law. How inherent this principle seems to be in our nature. From the moment a child knows what "no, no" means, he seems to prefer that over anything else available to him. Just let a sign of prohibition be erected and it becomes a challenge to some to violate it. Every law that is passed creates income for lawyers trying to find a way to circumvent it for their clients. The moment an order is given to us, something within rises up. We don't want to be told what we can and cannot do. We have indeed "turned every one unto his own way" (*see* Isaiah 53:6).

Usually (nearly 100 times) when we read the word *transgression* in the Old Testament, it is this Hebrew word *pasha', or rebellion.* Sin is rebellion—rebellion against God, His laws, His ways, His Word, and His will. Sin, or transgression, says, "I'd rather do it my way, no matter what the consequences." Rational? No. Rebellious! But such is the nature of sin that holds sway in the hearts and minds of this earth's population. No deterrent is strong enough, no revelation of the consequences vivid enough to deter us from sinning. It takes divine forgiveness to deal with the principle of rebellion before any man's behavior can be altered from bad to good. The *pasha'* must be removed. Defiance must give way to submission and obedience must replace disobedience, or our transgressions will eventually hail us into heaven's courtroom to stand before God the judge. What possible defense could we offer?

Most of us remember the pangs of conscience and deep feelings of guilt the first few times we gave in to our inner rebellion and transgressed the commands of God. But after repeated transgressions, these pangs virtually disappeared; not only that, but further sinning became easier. This perversion or distortion of our nature that is caused by sinning is represented by the word *'avah,* which literally means "to be bent or crooked." This original meaning of the word is shown clearly in Isaiah 21:3: ". . . I was bowed down at the hearing of it . . . ." It is translated variously in the King James as "desire," "lust after," "be desirous," "covet," "be perverse," "make crooked," "do perversely," "do wickedly," and "pervert."

What a picture of maturing sin! One of the characteristics of sin is that it is never fully satisfied and in its lust for more, calls for deeper involvements and more blatant rebellion against the given law. Dope pushers long ago learned to start with near-innocent, seemingly harmless forms of dope, patiently waiting until the person's system could no longer find satisfaction at that level. So it is with sin. Nearly harmless, innocent-looking transgressions only open the door to greater rebellion. Small tastes of sin eventually create an appetite for more and more until, like the life ruined by hard drugs, our life is twisted, bent, deformed, and perverted from what it once was. Decent people become so warped by sin as to become derelict. Regularly the news media gives us the story of the respected who became ruined. Sin, *'avah,* bends us.

But what is this empty, treacherous thing that causes us to violate trust, toss in confusion, break up and ruin lives, revolt against authority, and bend our lives crooked? What is sin?

The word translated "sin" throughout the Old Testament, with very few exceptions, comes from the Hebrew word *chatha,* which basically signifies "to miss the mark." Sin is a failure or a coming short of that purpose of life ordained by God. Since man was originally made in the very image of God, it must have been in the very fiber of his being to live as God lives, to want what God wants, and to will as God wills. Every departure from this is a coming short of the divine purpose in man's creation; it is a missing of the goal which should be reached.

This word does not suggest an inability to hit the mark, thereby leaving man without blame, but acknowledges guilt in coming short. Abilities were prostituted, a will was exercised wrongly, or full abilities were not utilized. What could have been done was not done, whether through carelessness or design. The mark is not missed through omission or inactivity, but by improper commission and activity. Sin, in the Old Testament concept, is not passive; it is always very active. Something has been done, but it has been done wrongly.

It is like the concert violinist who prefers to be a house painter, or the capable student who drops out of school. Sin causes man to miss the mark as surely as a champion skeet shooter will miss the clay pigeon if he points his shotgun toward the ground. God has a goal for man and originally gifted man to attain that intention. But sin caused man to settle for something far lower than God's designed purposes.

This same principle is taught in the New Testament, where the Greek word most frequently used for sin is *hamartia,* which, at least in classical Greek, meant "failure" or "to miss the mark"—as when a spear is thrown at a target but it falls short. It has also been used in classical Greek for missing a road, failing in a plan, or being frustrated in a purpose. As it is used in New Testament Greek, *hamartia* does not so much describe an act of sin (as does the Hebrew word *chatha* in the Old Testament) as it describes the state of sin which produces the act. It is obviously Paul's favorite word for sin, inasmuch as he used it over sixty times in his epistles. He so personalized sin that it could almost be spelled with a capital "S." Paul seemed to see sin as a malignant, personal power which has man in its grasp, and he used the word *hamartia* when referring to this force.

So sin, whether seen in the Old Testament or the New, is fundamentally a missing of God's mark for our lives. It is an intentional falling when we should have been standing or a taking a wrong turn on a properly marked road. But this is only the basic meaning of either *chatha* or *hamartia*. Sin is far more than mere failure, and the ramifications of being negligent to "press toward the mark for the prize of the high calling of God in Christ Jesus" (*see* Philippians 3:14) are far-reaching.

Consider a few things that the New Testament teaches us about sin. For one thing, it teaches us that sin is universal. This thing the New Testament writers called *hamartia* is not a form of spiritual smallpox, against which we may be vaccinated or from which we may recover, "For all have sinned, and come short of the glory of God" (Romans 3:23). Sin is to be found in the very best of men, not merely in society's worst examples of humanity. Everything the Old Testament tells us that sin is, the New Testament tells us is inherent in the nature of depraved man. Although it is terribly uncomplimentary, 1 John 1:8 says, "If we say that we have no sin, we deceive ourselves, and the truth is not in us." Sin is more common to man than fleas are to a dog.

But far worse than sin's universality is sin's authority. As the New Testament uses the *hamartia,* sin is a power that has men under its control as surely as the addict is under the control of drugs. A classic example of this projection is given in Galatians 3:22, which says, "But the scripture hath concluded all under sin . . . ." "Under sin" is a translation of the two Greek words *huph' hamartian.* Here the preposition *hupo* is in the accusative case and literally means "in dependence on, in subjection to, under the control of." Just as a child is under his parents, the laborer is under his boss, or the army is under its general, so we are under the control of, or in the power of, sin.

To reinforce this principle Paul uses several strong words

about sin's power. For instance, in Romans 5:21 he declares that ". . . sin hath reigned unto death . . ." and he uses the Greek word for a king. In Romans 6:14 he promises, "For sin shall not have dominion over you . . ."; or, more simply expressed, sin is said to lord it over us, for the word he uses for *dominion* is the Greek word for *lord*. In Romans 7:23 Paul speaks of sin taking us captive and uses the Greek word for taking a prisoner in war.

So forceful is the control of sin over man that Paul declares that sin dwells in man (*see* Romans 7:17, 20). It is not merely an outside force to be coped with, but it gets into the mind, emotions, and will of man until it occupies him as an enemy occupies a conquered country. Because of this, Jesus declared, "Whosoever committeth sin is the servant of sin," and Paul repeats this at least three times in Romans six (verses 6, 17, 20).

Remembering that the New Testament was written during the days of Rome's power, when the control of the master over the slave was absolute, we will better understand the violent authority sin has taken over men. Nothing in life belonged to the slave; he belonged to his master, body and soul. So great is sin's control over men today that, like Paul of old, no matter how much they may want to cease doing evil, they are under the control of an inner force which demands that they sin. Paul put it, ". . . for to will is present with me; but how to perform that which is good I find not. For the good that I would I do not: but the evil which I would not, that I do" (Romans 7:18, 19). How many men have said an "Amen!" to that.

So sin is a transgression, a missing the mark, a fall, an offense, a breach of truth, wretched wickedness, life-breaking evil, and open rebellion. But the New Testament adds to all this the fact that sin becomes a nearly personal power that exerts strong control in the life of the sinner. Its purpose is to ruin the man, and its end is death (*see* James 1:15). Once sin begins in our life, it cannot be stopped, although we may exert some control in how it may manifest itself. Stepping into sin is akin to launching a canoe in the rapids above Niagara Falls. No amount of paddling will keep the canoeist from going over the falls. The current is too strong, both for the sailor and the sinner. The flow of sin will eventually dash us over the falls, and few ever survive the experience.

Sin is man's mortal enemy. It cost man his Eden and separated the human race from fellowship with God. The curse of sin forced man to labor and to earn his living by the sweat of his brow. It was through sin that man was first introduced to discontent, hatred, violence, murder, sickness, pain, disease, and death. Sin clouded man's mind and replaced the truth with a lie. Sin caused man to take the throne of his life instead of letting Christ rule as absolute sovereign. Sin numbed our sensitivity to God, dulled our hearing of His voice, and blinded our eyes to His Kingdom. Sin has so separated man from the Spirit world as to convince him that he is only an animal, tied to his basic senses.

Earlier today I was reading while eating my lunch. I began to laugh out loud because of what I was reading. My big dog, Hezekiah, got up from my feet and began to nuzzle my hand, as if to ask what had excited me. I looked at the poor dumb animal and said, "You poor, limited beast. You cannot look at markings on a page and understand what another was thinking. You cannot look at other marks and interpret it as music. Your world is limited to your senses and instincts."

Instantly the Spirit breathed within me that sin has reduced man to a total incomprehension of God's realm very much akin to the limitations of a dog in the world of man. Man may sense and feel, but he cannot see and know. He rarely comprehends what he senses but reacts to it in simple instinct. What a price to pay merely to "turn every one to his own way" (*see* Isaiah 53:6), and yet man has been paying and repaying that price for untold generations.

Sin has indeed broken our contact with the Divine, has desensitized us to things spiritual, and consequently has so imbalanced us as to break our fellowship with others. Sin separates husband from wife, parents from children, friends from friends, and makes human associations increasingly difficult. It is certainly the destroyer of all that is good and needful in mankind.

But is it irreversible? Can its consequences be stayed? Is there any reprieve from its sentence?

Yes, praise the Lord, God has a complete answer for sin. He has handled sin as to its penalty, presence, power, and guilt. But the price is outrageously high. Can we afford it?

3

The Purchase of Forgiveness

"The soul that sinneth, it shall die" (Ezekiel 18:4, 20) is the theme of the Old Testament. It is not declared so much as a divine vengeance as it is revealed to be the ultimate end of all sin. When the New Testament introduces the concept of sin being an almost personal force that exerts complete control over our lives like the boss of a work gang, it tells us that this master pays wages: "For the wages of sin is death . . ." (Romans 6:23). Phillips translates this verse, "Sin pays its servants: the wage is death . . . ."

Whether we view sin as an act of violation (Old Testament) or a pact of vassalage (New Testament), each produces the same end—death! This is not merely a threat of a future sentence that is subject to the ruling of a judge as he studies all extenuating circumstances, but is an actuality at work daily in the lives of all sinners. We are not going to die; we are dying! We are now separated from God because of sin. ("But your iniquities have separated between you and your God, and your sins have hid his face from you, that he will not hear" [Isaiah 59:2].) Our bodies are decaying now because of sin, and even our enjoyment of life is

43

lost because of deep guilt feelings. The death that sin brings is a slow process, but it is eternal. Once it begins, it is never abated. Despite its unpopularity, hell is very real, and the Scriptures speak far more of the place of eternal torment than of the abode of the saints. Sin's death comes by degrees, and that which is suffered in this life is the smallest part of the price of sin; we could almost say that what we collect in this life is merely the interest on the wages that will be fully paid throughout eternity.

Recently I purchased a portable building and had it moved onto my property to serve as my study. After getting it all set up for writing, I discovered that during the time of storage, yellow jackets had built a nest in one of the light fixtures. As a measure of self-defense I purchased an insecticide, and when they began flying around the room, I sprayed them. At first I thought I had either purchased the wrong spray or had gotten an impotent can, for instead of dying, they appeared to become more active. But as I watched I noticed that they seemed to lose their sense of direction and would fly into things; then they lost their ability to fly, and next their ability to walk. Finally they died completely. I did not put them in the wastebasket until the process of death was completed, but the moment the spray hit them, they were as good as dead. Nothing they could do would change the workings of that spray. They died while extremely active, losing motor abilities one by one.

Such is the way of sin. Death is not instantaneous, but it is progressive. Even a small spray of sin will eventually extract the last breath of life from us. Once sin starts its work, the full penalty is unrepealable.

Because the only satisfaction for sin is death, no man can pay the penalty and survive. Whether we would give our life a ransom to be set free from sin or merely allow that sin to maintain its hold in us until our death date, the end result would be the same—"sin bringeth forth death."

Did God understand this when He created man as His crowning glory? Did He realize that sin would corrupt this "apple of his eye" (*see* Deuteronomy 32:10) and that this "living soul" (*see* Genesis 2:7) would lose that life and endure an eternity of death?

Of course He did. Sin did not catch God napping. Satan did not surprise God in Eden by introducing sin to Eve. God knew all along that this would (or could) happen. It was not because God lost control that sin entered the world, but because God was in control. Adam's fall did not cause God to switch to plan B; God has stayed with plan A all along. Although God the maker fully knew of man's inability to throw off the power of sin, He also knew of His eternal plan to put away sin (*see* Hebrews 9:26) once and for all. Although sin may have man out of control, it didn't even require an emergency council session in heaven. Sin was anticipated long before the world was created, and it was provisionally propitiated before man was ever made a living being. Similar to the father who takes out life insurance at the birth of his son to assure him an opportunity for college education, so God made very advance preparations to rescue man from the quicksand of sin.

Jesus spoke of these advance preparations in declaring that ". . . the kingdom [has been] prepared for you from the foundation of the world" (Matthew 25:34). In speaking of the ministry and persecution of the prophets who had been sent to declare God's way out of sin, He declared, "That the blood of all the prophets, which was shed from the foundation of the world . . ." (Luke 11:50).

Paul also declared that God's salvation from sin was part of the original plan in the creation of man, not a second thought or an emergency operation. In Ephesians 1:4 he wrote, "According as he hath chosen us in him before the foundation of the world, that we should be holy and without blame before him in love."

The writer of the book of Hebrews announced the same principle. In speaking of the rest God had prepared for His people, he writes, ". . . the works were finished from the foundation of the world" (Hebrews 4:3). Once God has planned and decreed a thing, it is considered as performed, even though there may be a span of time (by man's reckoning) between the design and the detail.

Peter quite clearly explained this when he wrote, "Forasmuch as ye know that ye were not redeemed with corruptible things, as silver and gold . . . But with the precious blood of Christ . . . Who verily was foreordained before the foundation of the world, but was manifest in these last times for you" (1 Peter 1:18–20). His mission was ordered before the world was made but was performed after man had been on this earth for thousands of years.

John the revelator affirmed this in speaking of the book of life: ". . . of the Lamb slain from the foundation of the world" (Revelation 13:8) and in telling of those whose names were written in this book of life ". . . from the foundation of the world . . ." (Revelation 17:8).

So we see that God's Kingdom involving men was prepared from before the foundation of the world. The prophets were commissioned from before the foundation of the world. We were chosen in Him before the foundation of the world, and all works necessary to allow us to enter into His rest were finished before the foundation of the world. Christ was foreordained as a Saviour, was declared the Lamb slain, and our names were written in the book of life before the foundation of the world.

It does extreme violence to the Word of God to suggest that Satan violated God's plan in the garden of Eden, thereby forcing God to make other preparations. The introduction of sin was not Satan's moment of victory over God; it was merely Satan behaving naturally, ". . . the devil sinneth from the beginning," 1 John 3:8 tells us. He was only acting consistent with his nature in the garden. Satan did not triumph—he only tried. Although man was disgraced, God was not confounded. He was prepared to redeem man out of the morass of sin and to restore him back into the image of God.

The Provision of Substitution

Ah! But what is this marvelous plan God had prepared before taking step one to create this earth? It is simply "The wages of sin is death" with one additional provision: substitution. God provided that the innocent could die for the guilty. The theologians call it vicariate; that is, done on the behalf of another. As we will later see, God illustrated this provision of substitution throughout all of the ritual sacrifices. He sought to establish in our minds that He was willing to accept the death of an innocent substitute as atoning for the sinner, providing he met certain qualifications.

Only death could atone for sin; only death could eradicate the sin principle; only death could erase the marks of sin; and only death could satisfy God's law concerning sin. There could be no shortcut, no lowering of the price, no bartering with God. Death and only death can answer sin. But God offered to accept the death of an innocent substitute. If anyone could be found who was holy, harmless, unimpeachable, pure, and righteous, God offered to accept the shedding of his blood instead of the blood of the sinful one.

But where could such a person be found? Various people of the earth have offered their virgin girls or their very young boys as human sacrifices to their gods, assuming them to be sinless, but we know that long before we can commit sin, we have a sinful principle at work within us. "There is none righteous, no, not one" (*see* Romans 3:10). We could search the world over and not find a sinless person among us. "For all have sinned, and come short of the glory of God" (Romans 3:23).

So although God has offered to accept the death of the innocent, there is no innocent one to be found in the world. Isaiah wrote of this conflict in saying, "And he [God] saw that there was no man, and wondered that there was no intercessor: therefore his arm brought salvation unto him; and his righteousness, it sustained him" (Isaiah 59:16). What man could not do, God did for man. Since man could never find a righteous man among his number, God became that righteous man in the person of the Lord Jesus Christ. It is put this way in 2 Corinthians 5:21; "For he [God] hath made him [Christ] to be sin for us, who knew no sin; that we might be made the righteousness of God in him." *The Living Bible* translates that verse as, "For God took the sinless Christ and poured into him our sins. Then, in exchange, he poured God's goodness into us!" Christ became the guilty, and we became the innocent. Christ experienced the wrath of God against sin, that we might experience the love of God eternally. Christ died that we might live.

But although it is done vicariously, it is not done for free. This pardon for sin, this forgiveness for all indebtedness against God and His law, cost heaven its crowned King. It required that "the Word [be] made flesh, and dwelt among us" (*see* John 1:14); that "Forasmuch then as the children are partakers of flesh and blood, he [Christ] also himself likewise took part of the same; that through death he might destroy him that had the power of death, that is, the devil; And deliver them who through fear of death were all their lifetime subject to bondage" (Hebrews 2:14, 15). Christ could not merely lower Himself to the status of an angel, for angels cannot die, and death is the price needed to ransom us from our sins. Hebrews 2:16, 17 reinforces this in saying, "For verily he took not on him the nature of angels; but he took on him the seed of Abraham. Wherefore in all things it behoved him to be made like unto his brethren, that he might be a merciful and faithful high priest in things pertaining to God, to make reconcilation for the sins of the people."

No puny mind of man can comprehend the price of God becoming man, but if we would try to imagine what it would be like to lower ourselves to the level of an earthworm, we would get a beginning concept of this first step in our redemption.

But perhaps becoming a man was the least part of the price. Having become man and having endured the rejection of the very ones He came to redeem (*see* John 1:11), Christ was actually made sin for us. On Calvary's cross, God laid on Jesus the sins of the whole world (*see* Isaiah 53:6). The sinless Son of God didn't have a chance to get used to sin, as we have. In one short span of time He had all of the iniquity, rebellion, tumult, power, and control of sin heaped upon Him—while He was in the midst of great physical pain and anguish. He experienced the darkness of sin, the separation from the Father, the shame that the departure of the glory of God always brings, and the deep inner conflict that tore at His soul.

Calvary was a tremendous price to pay for sin, especially for an innocent victim, but Jesus paid it all. From the cross there rang a cry that shook the very foundations of hell and produced shouts of joy in heaven. "It is finished," He cried (*see* John 19:30), and at that moment every price that God would ever extract for sin, every penalty that could ever be levied for violation of God's law, and every cent that was owed because of sin was paid in full. As Christ hung His head and died in the midst of darkness and anguish, sin's bondage was broken, sin's control over men was wrested away, and sin's power was negated. Sin became a caged, toothless lion, totally harmless if we stay outside the cage. The entire plan of redemption was finished. What God had planned, He had now performed. Men could now be fully forgiven because the price had been fully paid.

But although Satan lost the battle of Calvary, he still fights to keep that victory from becoming effective in the lives of believers. If he cannot keep us from accepting forgiveness, he will do his best to cloud our understanding of that forgiveness. Frequently he convinces us that we are only parolees and that one future violation will bring us back under the condemnation of all past sins. Other times he cons us into believing that we have only changed taskmasters and that God will extract far more service out of us than he ever did. But the Bible never hints at parole, or says that God has merely picked up our contract and that we are now indebted to Him. The Bible declares that we are a forgiven people. We have been redeemed in order that we might be free men in love with God.

If the purpose of Calvary was merely to purchase slaves for the service of God, heaven paid far too great a price. First, because most of us are very unprofitable servants— we require more than we produce. Second, God can create serving angels with His voice. Why would He pay the price of becoming a man, knowing sin, and dying just to get more workers? No, the price of His blood was to return man to the purity of Eden, so he could have fellowship with his God and again enjoy life. We have been forgiven in order that we might enjoy freedom from sin.

No wonder that the poets and the songwriters have tried repeatedly to adequately express the depth of love and the height of mercy shown at Calvary. Theologians admittedly cannot understand the cross, but the least educated can enjoy its benefits. But these benefits are not automatic. Christ's death did not set all men free. There are some conditions to be met before we are issued the receipt marked "paid in full."

4

The Preparation for Forgiveness

Before God became man there was a supernatural intervention that enabled barren Elizabeth to have a son. The father, Zacharias the priest, obeyed the instructions of the angel and called the son John. John was destined to be the forerunner who would prepare the way for the coming of Christ. The theme of his message was not what God was about to do but what God required man to do. To the crowds who came to him in the wilderness, John the Baptist cried, "Repent ye: for the kingdom of heaven is at hand . . . Bring forth therefore fruits meet for repentance . . . I indeed baptize you with water unto repentance" (*see* Matthew 3:2, 8, 11). His message seemed harsh and its requirements were severe, but when the one of whom he foretold arrived on the scene, Christ's message was the same.

"I came," He said, "to call . . . sinners to repentance" (*see* Mark 2:17).

Mark recorded the theme of Christ's early ministry: "Now after that John was put in prison, Jesus came into Galilee, preaching the gospel of the kingdom of God, And saying, The time is fulfilled, and the kingdom of God is at hand: repent ye, and believe the gospel" (Mark 1:14, 15).

Repentance, not vicarious substitution, was the theme of Christ's ministry, and after His resurrection He gathered the eleven disciples together and "Then opened he their understanding, that they might understand the scriptures. And said unto them, Thus it is written, and thus it behoved Christ to suffer, and to rise from the dead the third day: And that repentance and remission of sins should be preached in his name among all nations . . ." (Luke 24:45–47). From beginning to end Jesus preached repentance. In His final discourse with His close associates to whom would be committed the preaching of the Gospel, He connected repentance and remission of sins. Repentance precedes remission; it prepares the penitent to receive the remission. By virtue of the very nature of repentance it is impossible to receive remission of sins until repentance is produced.

Paul seemed to understand this priority, for in his defense before Agrippa he declared, "Whereupon, O king Agrippa, I was not disobedient unto the heavenly vision: But shewed first unto them of Damascus, and at Jerusalem, and throughout all the coasts of Judaea, and then to the Gentiles, that they should repent and turn to God, and do works meet for repentance" (Acts 26:19, 20). In his charge to the elders of Ephesus he said, ". . . I kept back nothing that was profitable unto you . . . Testifying both to the Jews, and also to the Greeks, repentance toward God, and faith toward our Lord Jesus Christ" (Acts 20:20, 21).

"Repent and turn to God . . . repentance toward God, and faith toward our Lord Jesus Christ." This is ever the order in the Scripture, whether in the Gospels, the historic book of Acts, the epistles, or the book of Revelation. This is not to be interpreted that repentance is more important or even equal with remission of sins, for repentance is wholly an act of man, while remission is completely a work of God. Nothing man can ever do can be put on the same level as that which God has done.

No, repentance is not on the same par with remission of sins, any more than a key is equal to the house it unlocks. Repentance unlocks the door of our life, thereby enabling us to receive divine mercy and grace. As long as we are closed and locked against God's forgiveness, even God Himself cannot and will not remit the guilt of our sins to Christ Jesus. The door to our will is locked from within, and only we have the key that can unlock it. It is called repentance toward God.

Aside from the fact that repentance is the one thing man must do to be forgiven, what is repentance?

Our English word *repent* is the translation of the Greek word *metanoeō,* which in classical usage meant "to change one's mind or purpose," or "to change one's opinion." As this and the noun form of it are used in the New Testament, they refer to a change of attitude toward sin and a shift of opinion that involves forsaking that sin. Repentance starts by being able to see sin as God sees it and reveals it in His Word, and then repentance accepts guilt for participation in sin and resolves to forsake it forever.

Repentance involves both a turning from sin and a turning to God. To only do the first may be reformation, but it is not repentance. To try to do the second without honest repentance is an attempt to approach God by our route rather than the way He has planned, and John 10:1 classifies such a person ". . . a thief and a robber."

The parable of the prodigal son is an impressive example of the double turning of repentance. Not only did this wayward son determine to forsake his miserable life by saying, "I will arise"; he completed his change of mind by saying (and doing) "and go to my father, and will say unto him,

Father, I have sinned against heaven, and before thee"
(Luke 15:18). Very likely he had changed his mind about his
choice of life long before this, but when he was willing to
couple a return to the father with his disgust for his state, he
afforded the father an opportunity to restore him to his
former status.

There is a social gospel which seeks to lift man out of the
mess sin has gotten him into, but it is not repentance, for it
does not direct man back to God the Father. It may change
men's minds about their state, but it does nothing to change
their minds about their standing before God. True repentance produces a double turning—from sin, unto God.

In some modern evangelism there seems to be a reversal
of cause and effect in the matter of repentance. A strong
emotional appeal is made and people's response to this
emotional stimulation is defined as repentance. But sorrow-
ful feelings, tears, and even remorse do not produce repentance, although deep repentance often produces all of these
responses. True repentance is a change of attitude, a
change of heart, a readjusting of the intellect. Repenting is a
mental act at the beginning. It is fundamentally a positive
answer to the facts of sin and the promise of redemption.

Jesus illustrated this in His parable of the landholder who
asked his two sons to help in the harvest. One refused, "but
afterward he repented, and went" (*see* Matthew 21:29). His
repentance was not evidenced with a great emotional display, nor is there indication that he even apologized to his
father; he merely changed his mind about the request and
changed his behavior to do his father's bidding. He had
another mind about the issue.

This is not to suggest that emotional outbursts are unusual or out of order. They simply cannot be called repentance. The day we learn the difference between repentance
and remorse may very well be the first day of victorious

living for us. I have dealt with many individuals whose
sense of remorse and sorrow for sin was so deep as to be
unsettling to their mental balance, and yet they often would
not repent, for that would require both a turning from sin
and a turning to God.

Simply stated, repentance first produces an intellectual
adjustment, second demands a volitional action, and third
may very well trigger deep emotional expressions.

Repentance is an inward act and should not be confused
with its fruits of confession, surrender, and restitution,
which are outward. When man has changed his mind about
his involvement with sin and his separation from God, it
will show itself in his outward behavior. But, again, we
cannot take the effects for the cause. Until there is a
genuine change of mind, confession is shallow, surrender is
hypocritical, and restitution may be little more than conscience salving. We do well to remember what the Lord told
Samuel: ". . . the Lord seeth not as man seeth; for man
looketh on the outward appearance, but the Lord looketh
on the heart" (1 Samuel 16:7).

But how beautifully positive this is. Before God can put
our sins on Christ's account and mark it "paid in full," we
must open ourselves to Him through repentance. He does
not ask for great outward show or for costly restitution. He
does not call for a signed contract or great pledges of al-
legiance. He merely asks us to change our minds about sin
and our relationship to God. How simple this is, and how
instantly it can be done. No outside priesthood is needed;
no church buildings are required. Wherever we are, whatever we have been doing, we are merely asked to do an
about-face in our thinking.

But while repentance may be fundamentally elementary,
it is far from easy. There is a deep-seated pride in each of us
that strongly resists a change of mind which admits we were

wrong and summons an armed guard to keep us from admitting another was right.

Recently while listening to the radio I heard a classic example of this. The speaker and his wife were traveling by auto to Detroit, Michigan. As he turned onto the expressway, his wife told him that Detroit was the other way.

"I know what I'm doing," was his curt retort, and for miles he nursed his resentment that she was backseat driving. When he saw a road sign saying "Chicago 75 miles," he was shaken up a bit but wouldn't accept the facts. After a second and a third road sign assured him that he was indeed headed for Chicago and not Detroit, he said that all his years of engineering training told him he was going the wrong direction, but his emotions insisted that he must find some way to get to Detroit without turning around.

If merely telling another person he was headed the wrong direction would produce repentance, the world would have been saved years ago. But even when we prove that the way he has taken is wrong and can never lead him to his desired destination, it still does not produce a change of mind and action. Insidious pride will cause him to continue to his own damnation rather than admit that he is wrong and God is right.

Although God made us rational creatures, sin has dulled our minds, blinded our eyes, desensitized our emotions, and filled us with pride. Generally, man will not repent! Frequently man cannot repent, for the power of sin is greater than the power of conviction. But repent we must, or we will die in our sins.

The Gift of Repentance

This is why God has made provision to bring repentance to the needy one. There is a principle throughout the Scriptures that declares that whenever God demands something in one place, He offers it to us as a gift in another portion of the Word. God knows we are too spiritually bankrupt to bring the required repentance, so He offers it to us as a gift. Acts 11:18 says, ". . . Then hath God also to the Gentiles granted repentance unto life." Repentance is not something which one can originate within himself, or can pump up as one would pump water out of a well; it is a divine gift. In speaking of the responsibilities of a servant of the Lord, Paul told Timothy that he should be ". . . apt to teach . . . if God peradventure will give them repentance to the acknowledging of the truth" (2 Timothy 2:24, 25). When Peter was speaking to the high priest and the council he said, "Him [Jesus] hath God exalted with right hand . . . for to give repentance to Israel, and forgiveness of sins" (Acts 5:31).

Although we are called upon to repent in order that we may feel our own inability to do so and consequently be thrown upon God to perform this work of grace in our hearts, we will need outside help. And that help is available in Christ Jesus. Nonetheless, we often do not understand this help when it comes, for we expect Him to do *for* us instead of giving *to* us.

God's gifts often come as processes; or to put it another way, God often alters circumstances to gently motivate us to do what He has commanded us to do. One of the first courses of action God uses to bring us to repentance is His goodness.

That God is inherently a good God none dare argue against, since it is so clearly declared in the Word of God (*see* Psalms 25:8). Yet while we give mental acquiescence to this truth, we more frequently carry a mental concept of God being the righteous judge of all the earth, waiting to sentence sinners to eternal damnation for breaking His law. Much of my early evangelistic ministry was predicated on informing people of impending doom, which could be averted only by turning to Jesus. But while I was neither unscriptural or unkind, I certainly was unaware that God's first approach to mankind is through His goodness.

In Paul's letter to the church at Rome he strikes a beautiful balance between the severity of God and the kindness of God. In condemning those who judged others while they themselves were guilty of the same actions, Paul asked them, "Or despisest thou the riches of his goodness and forbearance and longsuffering; not knowing that the goodness of God leadeth thee to repentance?" (Romans 2:4). The Greek word he uses here for *goodness* is *chrēstos,* which is the same word used in Matthew 11:30 for the yoke of Christ ("For my yoke is *easy* . . ."). It is a word used of things that are pleasant, and when used of persons is often translated as "kindly" or "gracious." It does not signify goodness simply as a quality, but goodness in action. It is goodness expressing itself in deeds. W. E. Vine tells us, in his *An Expository Dictionary of New Testament Words,* that *chrēstotēs* (the noun form) is "not goodness expressing itself in indignation against sin, for it is contrasted with severity in Romans 11:22, but in grace and tenderness and compassion."

So the first drawing to repentance comes from the gracious and tender deeds of God that express His compassion for sinful men. When He was talking to one of the rulers of the Jews, a Pharisee named Nicodemus, Jesus said, "For God sent not his Son into the world to condemn the world; but that the world through him might be saved" (John 3:17). Later in His ministry, after He had been rejected by most of the Jews, He amplified the statement by saying, "And if any man hear my words, and believe not, I judge him not: for I came not to judge the world, but to save the world" (John 12:47).

That He did not come to judge and condemn sinful man is evidenced by His behavior when He was God in the flesh. He broke up every funeral He ever attended by restoring the dead to life. He cleansed the lepers, unstopped deaf ears, healed the sick, cast out demons, repeatedly opened blind eyes, and restored the demented to complete sanity. He was gracious and tender to the women, whose plight was far worse than that of modern women, and He had time for the children and was loved by the men. He taught the unlearned, revealed divine principles to the spiritually hungry, and taught righteousness to those who lived in very unrighteous times. Repeatedly it is said of Him that "he had compassion on them," for He began to feel what they were feeling. He sat where they sat.

Peter, one of the twelve men chosen by Jesus to perpetuate the ministry Christ began, continually told of the good things Jesus did while He was here on earth. It was Peter who had denied Christ and received compassionate forgiveness instead of condemnation, and he never forgot that kindness. It was this goodness of God that had wooed him from fisherman to fisher-of-men, and it was this same goodness that won him back from denial to discipleship. His epistles abound with references to the preciousness of Jesus, to His availability to the seeker, to His redemptive work, to the great hope He brought, and to the inheritance He has left to us.

When Peter was preaching to Cornelius in Joppa, he told "How God anointed Jesus of Nazareth with the Holy Ghost and with power: who went about doing good, and healing all that were oppressed of the devil; for God was with him. And we are witnesses of all things which he did both in the land of the Jews, and in Jerusalem . . ." (Acts 10:38, 39).

And yet earlier in his relationship with Jesus, Peter had been among the disciples present when James and John pleaded with Him to call down fire from heaven to destroy those who seemed to reject Him. But as Peter matured, he realized that it was not by destructive fire, but by the warmth of love, that God had chosen to call men out of sin unto repentance.

This is not to be interpreted as free grace, which so often becomes disgrace. While Jesus did not condemn men for their sins, He did not condone their sinning, and whenever He touched their lives He lifted them out of their sins. But Jesus came to reveal the Father's love, not man's sin. Men knew sin, but they did not know God, who could lift them out of that sin.

When I was a young man still in Bible college, I was invited to be the speaker for a choir presentation in a large Southern California church on a Sunday morning. I prepared and preached a sermon on sin. I announced and denounced every form of sin I had any knowledge about and projected sufficient guilt that the altar call was very fruitful. While members of the choir were dealing with those who had come forward to pray, I returned to the school bus to await them. One by one they came, each praising me for a great message, when the pastor entered the bus with two of the students and asked, "Where is this morning's speaker?"

Expecting a small honorarium, or at least a plaudit, I quickly stood to identify myself, and the pastor came to me. Looking me squarely in the eye and speaking loudly enough for the entire bus to hear, he said, "Young man, don't kick the darkness. Turn on the light!"

With that he turned and walked out of the bus, leaving me humiliated. I thought him to be very ungrateful after I had gotten nearly half of his church saved that morning, but the more I mulled his words over in my mind, the greater they became. I wrote them in the front of my Bible, and I have repeated them to myself thousands of times since. "Don't kick the darkness. Turn on the light!" It was the finest gift any pastor has ever given me.

Christ did not come to kick the darkness. He said, "I am come a light into the world, that whosoever believeth on me should not abide in darkness" (John 12:46). He knew that no amount of preaching against darkness would rescue men from its power, so He came as a divine light; and when light comes in at 186,000 miles per second, darkness goes out at 186,000 miles per second. Christ still dispels darkness by bringing light.

That Christ was aware of the power of sin is evidenced in the fact that He wept over the sins of Jerusalem. He wept over them but did not talk about them. His message was not "how great is your sin," but "a redeemer is in your midst." He spoke out against inequities, injustices, and unfairness and taught principles of righteousness, but never in a condemning fashion. He always offered a positive way of response to whatever He preached, for He knew, far better than we do, that it is "the goodness of God that leadeth thee to repentance" (*see* Romans 2:4).

Perhaps one of the reasons God starts by being extra good to us is His knowledge that until a way of escape is revealed, few of us would ever admit guilt. Although the Viet Nam conflict had been over for several years, it was not until President Carter offered amnesty to military deserters that they began to return to the United States. They did not dare return while they were guilty, for there was hope of nothing but punishment. But when a way of escape was offered, even though it was limited and conditional, many of them took it.

So God first of all approaches us in love, with a gracious offer of amnesty. He ministers to us in a variety of ways and encourages us to trust Him to always be consistent with His revealed nature. This removes the horror and dread at having to repent, for we know repentance is an admission of guilt, and we must know that God will deal with that guilt in a way that is good for us, not destructive to us.

In counseling I have found this principle to be ignored by many believing, but sinning, Christians. As I have sought to help them see that their behavior was inconsistent with the clear teaching of the Word of God, they have denied any sense of conviction or dealings of God. As I have pressed the point of their sin further, they have frequently called as their defense some of the special giftings of God in their lives.

"God has never seemed closer," some have said.

"I've never had more prayers answered than during this time where it appears that I have been sinning," others have told me.

"I have never ministered with a greater anointing or more results," pastors have said defensively.

"The gifts of God are flowing more effectively now than ever in my life; how could I be guilty of sin?" many have asked.

But God's giving, His giftings, His graces, and His blessings are intended to bring us to repentance, not to pride. God does not come to us to enforce His laws, but to entice us into His love. He wants to lead us to repentance, not drive us to it. His first approach is to attract us with goodness, but if we will not come out of sin to repentance, He must attack us with chastisement, for He loves us far too much to leave us in our sin when all we need to do is repent to be lifted out of that damning sin. As with the woman Jezebel in the church of Thyatira, God gives us "space to repent" (*see* Revelation 2:21). When she did not repent, then God threatened tribulation (the Greek *thlipsis* means "affliction") to her and her followers.

During this space to repent God is extra kind, extra gracious and beneficent to us. He tries to help us see that everything we need is available in Him; we do not need anything that sin has to offer us. This "space" is almost like a honeymoon period. But it is God's longsuffering with us to bring us to repentance so that chastisement can be averted. If God cannot attract us, He will afflict us.

Godly Sorrow

Second Corinthians 7 beautifully illustrates this, for it is here that we learn how godly sorrow can also lead us to repentance.

Paul wrote, "For though I made you sorry with a letter, I do not repent . . . for I perceive that the same epistle hath made you sorry, though it were but for a season" (2 Corinthians 7:8). Godly sorrow is produced when our behavior is measured against God's Word and the Spirit causes us to know just how far short we have fallen. It is more than a consciousness of sin; it is a deep awareness of having violated our commitment to God and the pain we have caused both Him and others. In the case of the church at Corinth, they had long had a mental awareness that what was being done was wrong. When Paul's letter came, explaining how deeply it hurt God, Paul, the Gospel, and their testimony for them to allow that sin to go unchecked, it produced a response of grief, deep regret, remorse, and sorrow.

When the display of God's goodness fails to bring us to repentance, then God begins to show us our wretchedness. He does not threaten to cast us into hell; He merely reveals how cancerous our sin has actually become and how hideous it is in His eyes. Because of our love for Him, it often causes us to repent; that is, have a change of mind about our behavior.

My mother used to use this approach on me regularly. If

my behavior wasn't according to the code of the home, and her love and kindness didn't bring me around, she would have a talk with me.

"Judson," she would say, "you know that your father is the pastor of this church and the presbyter over the entire section. The way you are acting is a disgrace to him and to his ministry."

Usually that would bring me around, for I greatly respected my father and his ministry. To him it was not a profession—it was a life—and he lived in the home what he preached in the church.

I have moved my daughters to tears, in years past, by simply telling them how disappointed I was in them for behaving so contrary to the way they were reared. They so loved and respected me and so desired to please me that merely being informed that they had hurt me would produce sorrow in them that usually changed their behavior.

God moves upon ministers to so preach the Word as to make us aware that our lives do not please God. The Spirit quickens a passage of the Scriptures to reveal our sin and the sorrow it is causing others. Or the Lord may use a personal friend or even a casual acquaintance to put their finger on our wrong in such a way as to break our heart with regret.

This happened to me a few years ago. I had just recovered from a very lengthy sickness and still had not regained my full strength. Having been out of active ministry for over a year, I was having a little difficulty getting back into the mainstream of activity again. I felt I was being treated unfairly and was filled with self-pity.

The church I was associated with had a Thursday morning prayer meeting, and I put my pride in my pocket and attended in order to pour out my hurts and disappointments to the prayer warriors who, I hoped, would touch the throne of God in intercession, thereby causing God to change circumstances on my behalf. I must admit that I was very disappointed, upon my arrival, to be introduced to a minister from another state. Because of his presence I kept my request to myself for the first hour of the prayer time, but the inner turmoil finally exploded out of my mouth in the form of a plea for prayer.

The Christians and the local pastor were very solicitous to me and expressed great concern for the way I was being treated.

"Just a minute," the guest pastor called out across the prayer room. "Aren't you Judson Cornwall, who wrote the book *Let Us Praise?*"

"Yes, as a matter of fact, I am," I said.

"Then why don't you practice what you've written?" he asked. "You tell us in your book that we should praise God in spite of any circumstance, and you give illustrations of how you have come into great victories simply by praising. What's happened? Have you discovered that what you wrote won't work, or are you simply unwilling to take your own medicine?"

The local pastor jumped to my defense immediately, but I stopped him. The brother was right and was being used of God to reveal my sinfulness to me. I was a disgrace to the very Gospel I had preached and written about. My self-pity had blinded my eyes to the Lordship of Jesus. Things were not out of control; I was out of control. When I saw it, sorrow replaced pity and repentance came out of that regret.

Yes, God uses varied channels and methods to alert us to our sinfulness, and often He must use sorrow and remorse. But God's goal in producing sorrow is that the sorrow will produce repentance. In 2 Corinthians 7:9 Paul exclaimed, "Now I rejoice, not that ye were made sorry, but that ye sorrowed to repentance . . . ." In verse 10 he explained, "For godly sorrow worketh repentance to salvation not to be repented of . . . ." Other translations of this verse are even more poignant. "For God sometimes uses sorrow in our lives to help us turn away from sin and seek eternal life. We should never regret his sending it . . ." *The Living Bible* says. The *Amplified Bible* translates it, "For godly grief and the pain God is permitted to direct, produce a repentance that leads and contributes to salvation and deliverance from evil, and it never brings regret . . . ."

Because God is a good God, He does not keep us in pleasant circumstances when this seems to contribute to our departure from His ways. He who controls all circumstances of life can bring us both pain and pleasure, good and grief, happiness and hopelessness. It is an unfair oversimplification to credit to God all things we deem pleasant and to the devil all things we dislike. The woodshed experiences of my younger days were evidence of my father's genuine love, and the pressings, pains, griefs, and sorrows God deliberately sends into my life in order to bring me to repentance are good gifts, even if they are immediately interpreted as good grief.

Paying attention to a testimony service in any of our churches should reinforce the observation that no one comes to God because they want Him, but because they need Him. It is usually after grief, tragedy, sorrow, hurt, failure, or loss that people come to Christ. It took this to awaken them to their need of God. And it may take another application of negative situation to bring them to repentance later in their Christian experience. Sorrow is an effective tool of God that can bring us to repentance when everything else has failed.

Some years ago, when I was pastoring, I was involved in a practice that, if we face the Word of God squarely, is a violation of God's commandments. By the standards of the world it is quite accepted, but not by God's standards. Several times my conscience had been pricked and I had apologized to God, but in time I would get over the sense of guilt and would comfortably return to the practice. I could always rationalize that I knew other ministers who didn't seem to be bothered about doing it.

One day my study was interrupted by a knock on my office door. One of the women of the congregation, who had been in the prayer room for some time, stepped in and, quite unceremoniously, said, "Pastor, I don't have any idea what this means, but God said to tell you that this is the last time He will ever tell you to quit it. God is about to give up on you."

This was followed by an emotional apology and assurance that she didn't have any idea what it was all about. She hoped that she wasn't out of order. I assured her that as a messenger she had been faithful and that I did indeed know what God meant.

As I let her out of the office I slipped the lock on the door and dropped to my knees in prayer. I tried to repent, but my heart wasn't in it. I said all the right words, but nothing seemed satisfactory. Finally I said, "Lord, I just can't repent of this thing. Please give me a gift of repentance."

I wasn't prepared for what followed. God overwhelmed me with an awareness of how serious this thing was to Him and how it was hurting our relationship. With this insight came a sorrow and grief beyond anything I had ever known before. It was as though I was the greatest sinner in the whole world. I wept and prayed for several hours. At times I despaired of ever finding forgiveness, so deep was my sense of sin. All attempts to justify my behavior were gone. I only wanted forgiveness. That day of sorrow has left a deep impression on me. I so repented of that thing as to never want to be involved in it again. It became hideous and heinous to me. Certainly, ". . . godly sorrow worketh repentance . . . not to be repented of . . ." (2 Corinthians 7:10).

But not only does God's message produce sorrow and that sorrow produce repentance, but the sorrow-induced repentance also becomes very productive. Verse eleven lists seven products of this kind of repentance: ". . . ye sorrowed after a godly sort, [1] what carefulness it wrought in you, yea, [2] what clearing of yourselves, yea, [3] what indignation, yea, [4] what fear, yea, [5] what vehement desire, yea, [6] what zeal, yea, [7] what revenge . . ." (2 Corinthians 7:11, numbers added for emphasis).

When repentance has been caused by sorrow sent from God, it not only produces an acknowledgment of past failure but induces a change of behavior, so that there will not be a repeating of the offense. It gives us a holy hatred for that sin, and we treat it as a rattlesnake the rest of our lives. We share David's cry, "He brought me up also out of an horrible pit, out of the miry clay, and set my feet upon a rock, and established my goings" (Psalms 40:2), and we never want to return to that pit again. The rock of God's forgiveness feels so secure after sinking in the miry clay that we never want to leave it. Repentance that comes out of divinely induced grief is usually long-lasting. A price has been paid and the produce is appreciated.

But although repentance induced by sorrow has a permanence to it, it also has pain in it. It has grieved God and pained man. There is a far better way to be motivated to repentance: love for God. It was His love for us that first reached us; now our love for Him should produce immediate repentance for anything that violates our relationship with Him.

When Jesus was dining with Simon the Pharisee, Mary

came into the room and anointed Jesus with spikenard and washed His feet with her tears. It was a tremendous demonstration of love outpoured, but Simon found it very offensive because she had the reputation of being a sinner, likely a prostitute. Even the disciples declared the act to be a terrible waste. To help Simon put Mary's act in correct perspective, Jesus told him the story of a creditor who freely forgave two debtors, one of whom owed him five hundred pence and the other merely fifty. When Jesus asked Simon which debtor would love the creditor the most Simon answered, ". . . I suppose that he, to whom he forgave most . . ." (Luke 7:43). While admitting that this was an expected response, Jesus said to Simon, "Wherefore I say unto thee, Her sins, which are many, are forgiven; for she loved much . . ." (Luke 7:47).

For far too many years I accepted Simon's concept, not Christ's. I well remember some of us fellows discussing this in the dormitory at Bible college. We feared that because we had not been forgiven very much we would never be able to love the Lord with great depth. Two of that discussion group actually left school to go out into the world and taste of sin so they could be, as they supposed, more effective ministers. What a waste, for it was Simon, not Jesus, who gave us this formula.

It is not true that he who has been forgiven the most loves the most. I've met many who have been forgiven much who have very little love for God. They still harbor great guilts, have deep wounds because of their past sins, and attend church more as an avenue of escape from hell than as an expression of deep love for God. We do not fall in love with the forgiveness of Christ, but with the person of Christ, and we need not greatly violate that person in order to learn to love Him.

Perhaps in man's realm, great forgiveness produces great

love, but in God's realm, great love produces great forgiveness. The more intimately we love the Lord the quicker we will be to repent, and it is this repentance that brings the forgiveness.

Consider the young married couple just setting up housekeeping after their honeymoon. He comes home from work to find the table set with their wedding-gift dishes, candles burning, and soft music playing on the stereo. She has prepared a meal for her lover husband. But when she sets liver and onions in front of him, the magic spell is broken.

"I hate liver and onions," he says, pushing back his plate. "Don't ever serve it to me again."

Depending on his actions following that outburst, she may or may not go into a flood of tears and run from the room. But I'm reasonably sure that she will never serve liver again. Why? Because she loves him. Her deepest desire is to please him, and if he doesn't like liver, she'll never serve him liver again. That is true repentance. She has a change of mind about serving liver and thereby changes her behavior. The husband doesn't want her tears or expressions of deep remorse; he simply doesn't want liver.

So it is in our relationship with the Lord. He does not want to have to reduce us to grief and sorrow; He merely wants us to change our mind and actions to conform to His will. If we love Him, we will regularly repent of the little things that are annoying or displeasing to Him. The deeper the love, the deeper will be the confession and forsaking; hence the deeper will be the forgiveness.

Repenting should become as common to the Christian as breathing. We exhale the bad and inhale the good. We will breath out repentance and breath in forgiveness. We will rid ourselves of inward sin and receive, as the reverse and subsequent action, the righteousness of God.

5

The Phraseology of Forgiveness

So repentance is the key to forgiveness, and either God's goodness, godly sorrow, or our love for God will move us to repentance so that we may enjoy forgiveness.

But what, exactly, is forgiveness?

Picture the little boy who hurried home from Sunday school bursting into the house with excitement, shouting, "Mommie, I want to see my new blanket. What color is my new blanket?"

"I don't know what you're talking about," the mother said. "You don't have a new blanket."

"Oh, I must have," the little boy replied, "for my Sunday-school teacher told me that Jesus said it had come."

Not wishing to damage the boy's faith, but thoroughly confused at what her son meant, she quizzed him more closely as to what the Sunday-school lesson had been about.

"Well," the boy said, "my teacher said that Jesus would pray to the Father and that He would send another blanket."

Beginning to understand at last, the mother said, "You mean another comforter, don't you?"

"Yes," the boy replied. "Another blanket."

The boy was merely defining the word consistent with its usage in his little world. Just so, our comprehension of spiritual truths is limited by our grasp of the meaning we give to words, and when we are dealing with theological concepts, this can be very limiting and occasionally downright confusing.

Just as when defining an English word we will give synonyms and analogous words to help broaden the scope of meaning, so the Scriptures give us a variety of terms that unlock the vast storehouse of meaning for the word *forgiveness*. Let's take a look at some of these words, in alphabetical order, and then re-examine the word *forgiveness* itself.

One very important word is *atonement*. It is an Old Testament word that basically means "to cover." The Greek words used for it in the New Testament are sometimes translated as "mercy seat" and sometimes as "propitiation." It is used far more frequently in connection with the rituals of the Tabernacle and temple, showing how the sprinkling of the blood made a covering for the sins of man. Its basic concept is something which removes sin from God's view. It is not a hiding of that sin, but a removal of that sin. Therefore, it can be said that Christ has become an atonement for us. He has removed our sins from before God's eyes and we are viewed as sinless, for when our sins were laid on Christ, they were no longer on us. Forgiveness is more than a pardoning; it is a removal of sin from the life of the sinning one and the eyes of God.

Another term that is closely associated with divine forgiveness has been greatly popularized in the secular press during the past months. It is *born again*. Entire books have been written on this theme, and it is perhaps the most-used expression when Christians give their testimony of having received God's forgiveness.

Its two most notable usages in the New Testament are in the Gospel of John and the epistle of Peter. When talking to Nicodemus, Jesus declared, ". . . Except a man be born again, he cannot see the kingdom of God" (John 3:3). This raised immediate and perplexing questions in this learned man, but Jesus merely re-emphasized that it was as necessary to be "born from above" (marginal reading for "born again") and to be "born of the Spirit" (*see* John 3:5, 6) as it was to be born into the natural world. Peter told the early Christians the same thing that Christ had told Nicodemus. "Being born again, not of corruptible seed, but of incorruptible, by the word of God, which liveth and abideth for ever," he said (1 Peter 1:23).

The metaphor is vivid. Sin has so marred, scarred, and warped us that merely pardoning us would be grossly insufficient. We need a chance to start over. We need to be formed anew, to have a released spirit, a renewed mind, a guiltless conscience, and a God consciousness totally lacking in our sinful state. God chose to make us a new creature rather than to renovate the old creature, and that process is called being born again.

A third Bible word that illuminates the work of forgiveness is *cleansing*. In the Old Testament it is used with ceremonial washings of body, clothing, utensils, and houses. Its implication is obvious; things must be washed to be clean. In the New Testament the Greek word used is *katharizō,* from which we get our English word *catharsis,* which means "purgation." This word is applied to the cleansing of leprosy by Jesus and the cleansing of our sins by the blood of Jesus. First John 1:7, 9 teaches us, "But if we walk in the light, as he is in the light, we have fellowship one with another, and the blood of Jesus Christ his Son cleanseth us from all sin. If we confess our sins, he is faithful and just to forgive us our sins, and to cleanse us from all unrighteousness." When we confess sin we are more than excused for misbehavior; we are purged from that sin, cleansed from the filth and stain of that sin, and made as whole as the leper whose skin had returned to normal.

This, of course, is beyond the ability of man. The best psychoanalysis cannot remove the stain of sin. It may reduce the sense of guilt by lowering standards to fit the behavior, or may help us to project the guilt to another person or set of circumstances, but only God can actually cleanse us from the filth and pollution of sin. He who is forgiven by God is also thoroughly cleansed by God, for God cannot and will not have communion with a defiled saint, but He can and will cleanse him.

Very likely the second most common word used by Christians to describe the work of divine forgiveness is *conversion.* We often speak of our spiritual birthday as the date of our conversion, or speak of another whose life has shown a drastic transformation by saying "He really got converted!"

Both the Hebrew and Greek words which we have translated *convert* or *conversion* mean "to turn, to return, or to turn about." So when Acts 3:19 cries, "Repent ye therefore, and be converted, that your sins may be blotted out . . ." it is crying for an about-face.

Robert Baker Girdlestone reminds us, in *Synonyms of the Old Testament,* "The process called conversion or turning to God is in reality a *re-turning,* or a turning back again to Him from whom sin has separated us, but whose we are by virtue of creation, preservation, and redemption."

But we need to remember that while the confession of sins may be done as a volitional act of man, it takes a divine intervention to enable us to return to God. Jesus told us, "No man can come to me, except the Father which hath sent me draw him . . ." (John 6:44). Sin has so separated and alienated us from God that He must use His good offices to bring us back into fellowship; but He does just that. He converts us; that is, He turns us from sin unto Himself. He turns us from self-centeredness to a Christocentricity. He converts us from "children of darkness to light in the Lord" (*see* Ephesians 5:8); from rebels to saints; from sinners to sons. So great is the power of His forgiveness that our very nature begins to flow in a different direction, and things we once hated we begin to love, and vice versa.

A further forceful word associated with God's forgiveness is *justification.* Most laymen do not seem to realize that the words *justify, justification, righteous, righteousness, just, right,* and *meet* are all translations of the same Greek root.

Justification relates to man's position, not his condition. It is basically a change in a man's relation or standing before God. It has to do with relations that have been disturbed by sin, and these relations are personal. Man, once condemned, is now acquitted. Once under divine condemnation, he is now the subject of divine commendation. According to the language of the Scriptures it means to declare, or cause to appear innocent or righteous (*see* Deuteronomy 25:1; Romans 3:26). It is to reckon righteous (*see* Romans 4:2–8) or not to impute iniquity (*see* Psalms 32:2). To justify is to set forth as righteous. It is to declare one righteous in a legal sense. It does not deal directly with character or conduct, but with guilt and punishment.

Justification is securing a new reputation through Christ and being accounted righteous before God. It means far more than acquittal, for the repentant sinner receives back in his pardon the full rights of citizenship.

Justification is the result of the double imputation whereby our sins are imputed (given) to Christ and Christ's righteousness is imputed to us.

Kenneth S. Wuest, an eminent Greek scholar, writes in his book *Studies in the Vocabulary of the Greek New Testament,* "Justification in the Bible sense therefore is the act of God removing from the believing sinner, his guilt and the penalty incurred by that guilt, and bestowing a positive righteousness, Christ Jesus Himself in whom the believer stands, not only innocent and uncondemned, but actually righteous in point of law for time and eternity. The words *justify, justification, righteous, righteousness,* as used of man in his relation to God, have a legal, judicial basis. God is the Judge, man the defendant. God is the standard of all righteousness."

When we think of the forgiveness of God, we also think of our new legal standing before him. There is not one point of law that can be held against us, for Christ completely fulfilled that law, and He has become our righteousness. We have been justified—declared innocent—by Christ Jesus.

If you have ever had the joy of being present when a condemned man received a reprieve or when a convicted man was granted a parole, you know something of the unbounded joy that their new lease on life gave to them. But that is nothing compared to the joy the Christian has when he realized that in God's forgiveness he was granted neither a reprieve nor a parole, but has been declared not guilty, just, and righteous. He is not only saved from punishment; his reputation is fully restored and he is returned to life with no stigma.

Let us enjoy forgiveness. It is the basis for our whole new life in Christ Jesus and on this earth.

Used far more in our litany of worship than in the Scriptures is the word *pardon*. This is exclusively an Old Testament word and is not used by any of the New Testament writers.

Four separate Hebrew words are translated "pardon" in the King James Version, and two of these are only used once each. The word *nasa*, which literally means "to lift up," is used four times, and the word *salach* is translated "pardon" about a dozen times. Nonetheless, this same Hebrew word is used over thirty other times in the Old Testament, where it is translated "forgive." It would seem preferable for the word *salach* to be consistently translated "forgive" since pardon, as we generally use the word, does nothing to remit the guilt, but only the judgment. We think of a condemned man who has been convicted in the courts joyfully receiving a pardon from the governor. The pardon does not make the man guiltless; it simply revokes the penalty of the law and releases the man.

Forgiveness is not pardon in this sense. God will not—indeed He cannot—revoke the penalty of His law. He cannot, out of sheer magnanimity, set the condemned man free, as Pilate released Barabbas to the crowd. The justice of God demands that He be just and equal in His treatment of all men. He cannot punish some and release others. The full penalty of sin must be extracted. But while He cannot overlook sin, He can accept Christ's death as atoning for our sin and forgive that sin. Forgiveness deals with the sin; pardon, with the punishment.

A word that the Apostle Paul used widely in speaking of Christ's forgiveness is *reconciliation*. It is a strong and very active word, which is used in both Testaments of the Bible. The word in the original language of the New Testament is *katallassō,* and in classical usage it first referred to the exchange of money, then of something into money, and later to change from enmity to friendship, to reconcile.

Reconcile, in the New Testament, refers to the restoration of the relationship between man and God, with only two exceptions—one that refers to a wife returning to her husband, and the other that reminds us of Moses' attempt to stop the fight between two Israelites.

In Romans Paul declares, "For if, when we were enemies, we were reconciled to God by the death of his Son, much more, being reconciled, we shall be saved by his life" (Romans 5:10). This is the way this word is consistently used. Man is being restored to a harmonious relationship with his God. Man was created to share friendship and fellowship with God, but through his rebellious disobedience he discovered that he was no longer in intimacy with God, but at enmity with Him. We need to be very careful in understanding the teaching of the Word in this matter. Never once does the Bible speak of God being reconciled to men; it is always men being reconciled to God. "And all things are of God, who hath reconciled us to himself by Jesus Christ, and hath given to us the ministry of reconciliation; To wit, that God was in Christ, reconciling the world unto himself, not imputing their trespasses unto them; and hath committed unto us the word of reconciliation" (2 Corinthians 5:18, 19). It is ever man, and never God, who needs to be reconciled. Sin did not lessen God's love or turn that love to hate. It was not God who needed to be mollified, but man who needed to be moved from rebellion to repentance in order that he could receive love and love in return.

The work of the cross was to change not the heart of God, but the heart of man. William Barclay, an accredited authority on the Greek New Testament, wrote in *New Testament Words,* "It is entirely against all Pauline thought to think of Jesus Christ pacifying an angry God, or to think that in some way God's wrath was turned to love, and

God's judgment was turned to mercy, because of something which Jesus did."

The prime purpose of forgiveness is the restoration of a lost relationship. We have been forgiven so we can change our attitude from defensive anger to submissive love. We have been reconciled (made friendly, restored to fellowship) by God's outstanding demonstration of His consistent love, and Christ at Calvary is the apex of that manifestation.

The story is told of a servant caught stealing from the queen. She was brought before her majesty for sentencing. Throwing herself at the feet of the queen, the servant begged for forgiveness, pledging complete loyalty and trustworthiness in the future.

Touched by the tears, the queen commanded the servant girl to stand and look at her.

"I forgive you," she said, "but I don't ever want to see you again. Leave the palace and find employment elsewhere."

"But, your grace," the servant cried, "that isn't forgiveness; that's pardon. I want to be forgiven, so that I may remain in your service."

Surprised at the depth of the servant's understanding and realizing the paradox of qualified forgiveness, the queen said, "You're right; that wouldn't be forgiveness. Return to your duties as though nothing had happened, for I declared that I forgave you."

God did not send Jesus into this world merely to give men an escape from hellfire and damnation. Christ came to reconcile us back into the love relationship Adam had with God in the garden of Eden.

Another euphemistic term for forgiveness that is used far more in the pulpit than in the Bible is *regeneration.* The Greek word so translated is *paliggenesia,* which is actually a combining of two separate words: *palin,* an adverb mean-ing "back again," and *genesis,* a noun used in the New Testament in the sense of "origin, race, birth." Simply stated, regeneration means "a recreation," or "to be born again." It alludes to mankind having lost the divine life of God as it was given in Adam and as needing a second impar-tation of that life through the *paliggenesia,* the new birth. This, of course, is exactly what God's forgiveness provides.

But without question the most important word that helps us to understand God's forgiveness is *salvation.* The Greek word is *sōtēria,* which has a wealth of translatable truth. As used in the Greek text of the Old Testament, it means "gen-eral safety and security, deliverance from trouble in gen-eral, or deliverance from an enemy." In the New Testament its meaning is expanded to include bringing men back into a harmonious relationship with God. It teaches that only Jesus can save and that it is the will of God to save, not damn, men. Salvation is viewed as: past—in God's plan and Christ's purchase; present—in our acceptance and enjoy-ment; and future—in our eventual abiding with God in heaven.

The very concept of being saved raises the question, "What is man being saved from?" Beautifully God's for-giveness saves man from physical illness, for salvation is concerned with man's triune nature, spirit, soul, and body. It saves man from sin, with its infectious power and all of its consequences. It saves man from his "lostness" and brings him back into fellowship with both God and other Chris-tians. Of course it saves man from the wrath of God and the incumbent fear of God. It saves man from wasting himself on something far beneath God's plan for his life. It saves man from the guttermost to the uttermost and gives him an entirely new life. No wonder it is referred to as "so great a salvation" (*see* Hebrews 2:3). Someday, perhaps soon, forgiven ones will stand in heaven and shout, ". . . Alleluia; Salvation, and glory, and honour, and power, unto the Lord our God" (Revelation 19:1).

If there is one central theme to be seen in reading the many Scriptures that contain the word *forgive,* it is that God wants to forgive. It is a natural expression of His love. We need not try to talk God into a forgiving attitude; forgiveness is consistent with His nature. It is as natural for God to forgive as it is for a sparrow to fly or a fish to swim. There is no limit to His pardoning love, except blasphemy against the Holy Spirit (*see* Matthew 12:32), but that forgiveness cannot be extended to man until repentance is offered.

Paul quoted David's appraisal of God's forgiveness when he wrote, "Even as David also describeth the blessedness of the man, unto whom God imputeth righteousness without works, Saying, Blessed are they whose iniquities are forgiven, and whose sins are covered. Blessed is the man to whom the Lord will not impute sin" (Romans 4:6–8). Forgiveness is more than the removal of sin; it is the reception of imputed righteousness. It is more than escaping judgment; it is embracing justice. It is a stepping out of the banishment of God, into His blessings.

Once we have overcome the pain to our pride that confessing produced, we cannot help enjoying forgiveness. It is everything we had ever longed for, and more, because the painful process of repentance quickly gives way to the pleasurable process of forgiveness.

6

The Process of Forgiveness

As we well know, much of the language of the Bible is actually picture language. Spiritual truths are told in graphic form, which causes us to associate common occurrences as immediate illustrations of the principle. It enables us to proceed from the known of our little world into the unknown of God's world with some understanding.

In addition to this, God has recorded many happenings in the lives of others as His visual aids to make divine teaching vivid and understandable. Of the children of Israel, Paul declared, "Now all these things happened unto them for ensamples: and they are written for our admonition, upon whom the ends of the world are come (1 Corinthians 10:11). Long before man had mastered the art of writing, God knew the value of simple illustrations, for they are like windows that let the light in so we can more easily comprehend the contents of the room.

Repeatedly God has used this kind of language and multiple illustrations to help us grasp the breadth and the comprehensiveness of His forgiveness of sin. Only by looking at these pictures, and the words the writers chose to use to

describe them to us, can we get even a partial understanding of the process of forgiveness. What really is involved in
God's forgiving man? How does it work?

Of the multiple examples of forgiveness given in God's
Word, three of them seem to illustrate the process better
than the rest, and they are repeated throughout the pages of
the Scripture. The first of these is the concept of *buying
back.*

Because of the popularity of the book of Ruth we are,
perhaps, more familiar with the *goel,* or kinsman-redeemer,
whereby God made it possible for a Hebrew to buy back, or
redeem, property he had pledged as a loan and had lost. The
inheritance of land was a vital part of maintaining family
lines, so property that was sold automatically reverted to
the original owner or his heirs in the year of Jubilee. This
was the year of release, or the year of redemption, when all
slaves and indentured servants were released as free men
and women and all property was released from incumber-
ances. Nonetheless, this year occurred but once each fifty
years, which meant that for many people it would not come
in their lifetime. If property were pledged as payment for a
loan or sold outright, it could be redeemed any time the
original owner or his heirs could afford to pay back the sum
of money involved.

However, if (as in the case of Ruth and Naomi) the heirs
could not afford to repurchase the land that had changed
ownership, a close relative, known as a kinsman-redeemer,
could purchase it for them and give them free title to it. This
was what Boaz did for Naomi, and then he married Ruth.

What a glorious picture of the redemptive work of Jesus
on our behalf! Our sin cost us title to the inheritance God
gave to mankind through Adam. Like Elimelech and Ruth,
we were forced out of our pleasant places and had to
sojourn in a strange land. Every attempt to amass enough
possessions to redeem what had been lost failed, for there is

nothing a man can give as a ransom for his soul (*see* Psalms 49:7). Man's control over nature was reversed, leaving him a prey of nature and frequently subject to its whims and elements. Man's mastery over himself was bartered away, and he found himself under the control of strange and hostile powers over which he could only temporarily prevail. Man's rich fellowship and communication with God was broken, and man found himself a stranger on this earth.

In spite of all the promises, it seemed that man's year of Jubilee would never come. But these promises kept a spark of hope alive that someday, somewhere, God would send a *goel*—a kinsman-redeemer.

This hope came out of the lips of distressed Job as he cried, "For I know that my redeemer liveth . . ." (Job 19:25). I realize that there are divergent views as to what Job meant by this ecstatic expression, but whether it was a prediction of a coming Messiah; an early declaration of the doctrine of the resurrection; or merely an expression of his faith that a temporal deliverance from disease and trouble would come, it is obvious that Job expressed his deep conviction that there was a living God who could and who would take his part and deliver him from his difficulties. Job saw the ministry of a kinsman-redeemer before the law ever made such a provision.

David, too, saw God as his redeemer—his *goel*—and credited Him with deliverance from temporal as well as spiritual ills (*see* Psalms 19:14; 49:15). Whenever a circumstance was beyond David's ability to handle it, he turned to God to redeem him out of it, for he saw God as able and willing to get him out of whatever mess he or others had gotten him into.

Another function of this next of kin was to avenge the blood of a murder victim. If one of his near relatives was slain, he was allowed to seek out and slay the killer as vengeance (*see* Numbers 35). What a foretelling of the one

who would thoroughly avenge the blood of His brethren
that was shed by the one Jesus declared "was a murderer
from the beginning" (*see* John 8:44). It was not pacifism
that caused Paul to write, "Dearly beloved, avenge not
yourselves, but rather give place unto wrath: for it is written, Vengeance is mine; I will repay, saith the Lord" (Romans 12:19), but a deep awareness of our inability to avenge
ourselves. This is the expressed duty of the *goel,* the
redeemer—and how beautifully He did it on Calvary's
cross, and shall continue to do it until we are fully united
with Him eternally.

So in the concept of the *goel,* forgiveness is pictured as
God buying back what we had allowed to be taken from us
or had lost through our bartering with sin. But wherever we
see the *goel* functioning, we are made aware of a close
relationship between the redeemer and the one who will
benefit from the redemption. It is never merely a redeemer;
it is a kinsman-redeemer. This provision was probably
made as a foreshadowing of the incarnation of Christ, who
had to be made our kinsman before He could redeem us.
Paul spells this out quite clearly in Galatians, where he tells
us, "But when the fulness of the time was come, God sent
forth his Son, made of a woman, made under the law, To
redeem them that were under the law, that we might receive
the adoption of sons" (Galatians 4:4, 5). Christ became our
next of kin both to redeem back everything we had lost and
to restore us to a sonship relationship with God.

It might be well to note that there were four conditions
that had to be met for the work of the *goel* to be effectual.
First, he must be the nearest living relative qualified to
redeem. Second, he must be able to redeem without bankrupting his own resources. Third, he must be willing to
redeem the relative, since it contributed nothing to his own
possessions. Fourth, his work of redemption must be asked
for.

Through the incarnation, Jesus became our nearest living relative; so near, in fact, that Ephesians 5:30 declares, "For we are members of his body, of his flesh, and of his bones." The relationship was established entirely by God Himself. We could do nothing to be so closely related, but He could and did.

As for God's ability to redeem us, the entire Bible attests to that. There is nothing beyond the power of God. He can redeem every man, woman, boy, and girl on the face of the earth from now into eternity without bankrupting heaven's resources. And certainly God is willing to redeem. The first Bible verse learned by many of us teaches us, "For God so loved the world, that he gave his only begotten Son, that whosoever believeth in him should not perish, but have everlasting life" (John 3:16). So He is qualified, able, and willing. He only awaits our petition, which, we have learned, is repentance. When we repent at having forfeited it all, He is ready to restore it all back to us with no strings attached.

The process of forgiveness, then, is more than saying, "I forgive you." It is a buying back of that which is rightfully ours and a receiving back of that life that had been murdered by Satan and sin. It is a cancellation of all contracts that were outstanding against us in the moral realm and a returning of us to our rightful place in the family of God. All that our heavenly Father had given to us in His will and testament (both the Old and New Testaments) is restored and warranted unto us when Christ forgives us of our sins. No wonder we should enjoy forgiveness!

Redemption and Ransom

But there are other pointed illustrations of *buying back* that God uses to illustrate how His forgiveness works. One of these pictures is the use of the silver coin of redemption to purchase back the firstborn sons. In Exodus 13 God declared His ownership of all firstborn, both of the beasts and of mankind. Since He spared their firstborn in Egypt when He slew all the firstborn of the Egyptians, God declared his ownership over them. Still, God made these available to the owner or parents. For a specified substitution (a lamb in the case of a beast and a silver coin in the case of a son) the dedicated or devoted thing could be transferred back to the giver. This process was called redeeming, and the coin came to be called the redemptive coin.

Nothing had to be redeemed, but if the owner chose not to redeem an animal, its neck was to be broken. It could not be used. The unredeemed son would forever be dedicated to the menial service of the tabernacle, totally cut off from normal life without any of the benefits of being in the priesthood. That which was unredeemed was cut off from functional living.

All of us, in our first birth, deserved to have our necks broken, or at best, be set aside from enjoyment of life. We came into this world with no rights of our own and no title to a fulfilled life. But God! In mercy beyond our wildest imaginations, God sent His own Son as the Lamb of God to become our substitute—a redemption—so that we could escape the sentence of death and could live fulfilled lives. The death we were destined to die became Christ's death so that we could live His life to the very fullest. Jesus told His disciples, and us, ". . . I am come that they might have life, and that they might have it more abundantly" (John 10:10), and, "These things have I spoken unto you, that my joy might remain in you, and that your joy might be full" (John 15:11).

So forgiveness is also pictured as being bought back from a certain death. This death is not because of some violation on our part; we are devoted to death before we come forth from the womb. But Christ Jesus became our redemption in

His death as the Lamb of God. No wonder the book of Revelation refers to Him under this title repeatedly and with great awe. In order to restore our opportunity to live life, Christ had to give His life. But He did just that and in doing so, "Christ hath redeemed us from the curse of the law, being made a curse for us: for it is written, Cursed is every one that hangeth on a tree" (Galatians 3:13). *The Living Bible* translates the first portion of this verse, "But Christ has bought us out from under the doom of that impossible system . . . ." Born for slaughter, we have been saved for subsistence. We have been bought out by His generous redemption.

There is still a third, and very powerful, illustration of how God's forgiveness works connected with this concept of buying back, and that is in ransoming another. Jesus declared, ". . . the Son of man came not to be ministered unto, but to minister, and to give his life a ransom for many" (Matthew 20:28), and this is attested to in 1 Timothy 2:6, "[Christ Jesus] Who gave himself a ransom for all . . . ."

We must realize that the whole background to the word *ransom,* both in Greek and in English, is "captivity." It is always concerned with retrieving, emancipating, freeing, or liberating a person or a possession from some hostile power that has taken possession of him or it. With the great wave of kidnappings we have been experiencing in recent years at the hands of terrorists throughout the world, we should quickly grasp the meaning of being ransomed. An innocent person, and often one who is totally uninvolved, is captured by force and hidden. The terrorists offer to release the victim for certain concessions by the government, or in exchange for the release of some of their imprisoned members, or for vast sums of money. Unless these terms of ransom are met, the victim is killed and his body left in a place where it will be discovered and become a warning to all that these terrorists are not to be trifled with.

When we speak, then, of Christ's having given His life as a ransom, we must first recognize that a powerful and sinister force—sin—had taken us captive and secreted us from the presence of God. It did not necessarily require any involvement on our part; we were merely captured while going about the everyday duties of life. But once seized, we were totally cut off from our former way of life. We became prisoners, totally subjected to the commands of our captors. Our life was in constant jeopardy and we lived in fear. Quickly we learned that there was absolutely nothing we could do to set ourselves free. If others did not come to our rescue, we were doomed.

But rescue came! Christ "gave his life a ransom for many" and in doing so, paid the price asked; exchanged His life for ours; ransomed us from our captor, sin. But at what a cost! It was, again, life exchanged for life—His for ours. We were ransomed, rescued, and released by one who submitted Himself to capture, torture, and murder. Our freedom was effected by His captivity, our release from the torment of sin by His torture of sin; and our restoration to life was arranged by His substitutionary death. How greatly God loves us to forgive us at such a price.

Sometimes, nonetheless, the kidnappers seem to brainwash the captive into believing that their cause is just, and thereby they gain the volitional involvement of the kidnapped in the kidnapping, as might have been the situation in the celebrated Patty Hearst case. Far too many captives of sin become partners in sin, falsely believing that God's way of purity is suspect. Eventually they discover their deception, but usually it is too late. They have sinned away their day of redemption by refusing to be ransomed. How aggravated will their misery in hell be when they realize

that, at no cost to themselves, they could have been released from the overwhelming power of sin.

The verb form of the Greek word the New Testament
translates as "ransom" is *lutron,* and it is consistently used
in the Septuagint (a Greek New Testament) of God's redeeming of Israel from slavery in Egypt. This mighty act of
ransoming or rescuing an entire nation from captivity is
often used in the Old Testament as a measurement of God's
divine power. Israel was commanded to remember her release, and the Passover was instituted as an annual com-
memoration of the finality of that deliverance.

For over three hundred years Israel had been bondmen to
Egypt, but God sent them a deliverer in the person of
Moses and deliverance through great signs and wonders.
They were ransomed back to freedom; they were redeemed
from captivity by the overwhelming power of God, who not
only released them but gave the captors a strong taste of
what they had been giving to the captives for several cen-
turies. Their freedom was restricted by darkness; their
luxuries were removed by turning their water supply into
blood and covering their land with lice and frogs. Their
cattle and crops were destroyed, and their sons were slain.
Just as the kidnappers at Entebbe were not paid, but slain in
order to release the captives, so Christ has also effected the
release of sinning man by effectively reducing the power
of the enemy to zero. Satan has been overpowered by
God's might and must release his captives upon God's
command.

We who were born to slavery, we who had never known
the joys of being free from sin, have been ransomed, redeemed, delivered from our bondage both by Christ's paying the price and by God's destruction of Satan's power.
We have been freed from the captivity of the past and any
subsequent fear of future captivity. We've been emanci-

pated and avenged, all through the operation of God's forgiveness.

Repayment

So the first major example of the process of forgiveness is a buying back. Similar to it, but differing in some ways, is the picture of *paying a debt.*

There is a beautiful picture of Christ paying our debt for us in the short book of Philemon. The reason Paul wrote to this fellow Christian was to intercede for a runaway slave who belonged to Philemon. Somewhere, this slave had crossed Paul's path and had accepted the Lord Jesus Christ as a personal Saviour, and then had remained to serve Paul. Now Paul has urged him to return to his master and to serve him as though he were serving the Lord himself.

To help pave the way for the return, Paul wrote to Philemon, urging him to receive Onesimus not as a servant but as a brother and then said, "If he hath wronged thee, or oweth thee ought, put that on mine account" (Philemon 18). Paul simply guaranteed settlement of any indebtedness this slave may have occasioned before becoming a Christian. "Charge it to me," Paul said.

This is exactly what the Lord Jesus has declared concerning every slave who has come to Him. When former taskmasters seek to recover what they feel is owed to them, the Lord simply writes, "Charge that to Me. Put it on My account."

When old habits that once enslaved us begin to demand that we "pay up or else," we can simply remind that old master that Christ Jesus said, "Put that on My account." When guilt raises its ugly head, threatening us with lawsuits because of our past behavior, we can tell all of that inner guilt that Jesus said, "Put that on My account." The forgiveness of Christ fully cancels all of our indebtedness to sin by paying the price for us, thereby leaving us with a clear account.

It is very much like loaning your gasoline credit card to someone leaving on a trip. They will incur the debt and receive the goods, but you will pay the account. Or it is similar to accepting the charges on a long-distance phone call. The other party made the call, but its cost will appear on your bill. Jesus simply said, "Bill their sin to Me."

But this is a difficult concept to accept, for most of us Christians carry a load of guilt that produces anxiety, destroys our zest for life, and hinders our walk in God. We are aware of the consequences of past sins and somehow pick up a heavy responsibility for alleviating them. We believe that God has saved us, but we still feel that we have to make up some of the bad past. But in doing so, we are totally overlooking the truth that "Jesus paid it all." He insisted that it all be charged to His account. We have come out of sin completely free of any obligations to the past, and all of sin's claim over us has been broken once and for all because Christ Jesus has accepted full responsibility for all of our past behavior and its consequences. He does not send us back to straighten things out; He simply says, "I'll pay the damages. Come, follow Me." That makes it easy to enjoy forgiveness.

But an even more powerful portrayal of Christ paying a debt for us is the one Paul paints in Colossians 2:13, 14 where he says, "And you . . . hath he quickened together with him, having forgiven you all trespasses; Blotting out the handwriting of ordinances that was against us, which was contrary to us, and took it out of the way, nailing it to his cross."

It is very likely that Paul was alluding to a rather common practice of the moneylenders of his day. When a debtor entered into a contract with a creditor, the transaction was written up on papyrus and signed, very much as we do a personal note today. Then the document was torn in half with as jagged a tear as they could make. Half of the note was kept by the lender and the other half was given to the borrower, who was required to post it on the outside doorpost of his home to let everyone know that he was in debt. It was an early form of the credit reports that businessmen subscribe to today in their effort to avoid bad credit risks.

When this debt was paid, the debtor took his half of the contract to the creditor, who then matched it with the piece in his files that perfectly meshed with the uneven tear and marked it paid in full. This entire contract was then posted on the front door of the debtor as proof to all visitors that he had paid his account completely and owed no man.

If, however, the debtor was unable to pay his indebtedness and another was willing to pay it for him, the provision was somewhat different. In this case it was the benefactor who took the debtor's part of the note to the creditor and paid it off. He was given the canceled two halves but was not allowed to post it on the door of the friend. He must now display it on the post or bulletin board in the public square of the town. Everyone now knew that the debt was settled but that it had taken the intervention of a philanthropist to do it. It alerted the business world to the settling of the account and to the fact that the man was a poor credit risk, for he could not pay his own contracts.

What a vivid picture of the forgiving grace of Christ Jesus our Lord. Our portion of the contract of sin was posted on the doorpost of our life in full display for all to see. Although it was not discussed, it was common knowledge that we were deeply in debt and that the due date was coming up. There was no way we could pay the debt for, as we have learned, only death could fully settle the sin account. Then one day the blessed Son of God asked us if we would allow

Him to pay the debt in full for us. When we surrendered our portion of the contract into His hands, He paid the creditor everything that we owed and then nailed the fulfilled contract to His cross in full display to heaven, earth, and hell that we were no longer in debt to sin. It was paid in full.

But Paul adds one additional detail that further illuminates God's goodness in forgiving us. He says, "Blotting out the handwriting of ordinances that was against us . . ." (*see* Colossians 2:14). The more common Greek word for the cancellation of a contract is *chiazein,* which means to write the Greek letter *chi,* which was the same shape as a capital X, right across the document. This was called a "cross out." But Paul uses the Greek word *exaleipheim,* which literally means "to wash over," as in whitewashing, or "to wipe out." The ink used in Paul's day was basically soot mixed with gum and diluted with water. It would last for a long time and retain its color, but a wet sponge passed over the surface of the papyrus could wash the paper as clean as it had been before the writing had been inscribed on it. This is the word Paul uses here. Our sins have not merely been canceled out; they have been blotted out. Before our contract was displayed on Christ's cross, He mercifully wiped it totally clean, leaving no indication of past involvements or sins. Our name at the top of the page and the notation "paid in full, Jesus Christ" is all that remained. The rest of the page is fresh and ready for use again.

God made this truth tremendously clear to me when I was pastoring on the West Coast. I had been burdened for a pastor who had been defrocked by his denomination for immorality and had moved to my community to start life over as a watchman for a plywood mill. Over a period of many months, we lunched together and came to know each other quite well. I continuously sought to cause him to accept the forgiveness he used to preach and encouraged him to live as a forgiven man, but it was difficult for him, since he had lived most of his life in the concept that God has a separate standard for ministers. After more than a year, the reality of God's forgiveness began to dawn upon him. He and his wife attended our church, and he occasionally ministered for me. It was great to see this guilt-ridden brother begin to accept the fullness of God's glorious forgiveness. In time, his denomination recognized the change in him and reinstated him, offering him a small church to begin his ministry anew.

The day he was to leave to accept this new charge, I phoned him on his job to assure him of my continued interest and prayers, only to be informed that he had changed his mind.

"Why?" I inquired. "I thought it was all settled."

"Judson," he said, "I just can't go through with it. After what I did in my last church, I don't deserve another chance. I'm not worthy to preach the Gospel of Christ anymore."

Shocked and disgusted, I hung up on him and went directly to the prayer room in the church.

"Lord," I prayed, "have I been mistaken about him all along? Did he really confess his sin, or did he merely admit his guilt? Is he caught up in self-condemnation, or is he still guilty in your sight?"

God's answer came in the form of an immediate vision. With my eyes still closed in prayer, I saw myself in a large room that had bookcases on all four walls with volumes of leather-bound books from floor to ceiling. It reminded me of a legal library. As I looked at the books, I saw that they were alphabetized by names of people. A large hand with an extended index finger began to move across the books, until it came to the one with this minister's name on it. The book was removed from the shelf, placed on a small table, and opened in such a way that I could see and read the pages.

The first page told the story of his birth, and subsequent pages told of his early childhood, of his call into the ministry while he was still in his teens, of his first ministry and pastorate, of his courtship and marriage, and of his climb to a respected position in his denomination. I could only wish I possessed the ability to read as rapidly in real life as I was able to read in that vision. Everything that I read fit what I had come to know about this man.

The top of each page was dated, very much like a diary, and as the pages got closer and closer to the first incidence of adultery, I wondered how God would have it recorded. But when the book opened to that date, the page was absolutely blank, as were succeeding pages for what would be chapters of space. Then when we came to the date of his repentance, it was fully recorded with a marginal gloss that this had produced great rejoicing in heaven. Following this, the pages recorded his progress back into faith, his ministry in our church, his reacceptance into the denomination, and his call to the new church. Puzzled by the many blank pages, I asked if I could have a closer look at them. My request was granted, and I saw that there had been writing on the pages, but that it had been erased. On the bottom of each erased page, in red, were the initials "JC."

True to his word, Jesus Christ had "blotted out the charges proved against you, the list of his commandments which you had not obeyed . . ." (Colossians 2:14 LB). Heaven had no record of this man's sin. The only existing record was in his memory.

Excited with this revelation, I rushed to the phone and called the brother. After I told him what God had shown me, he quit his job, took the church, and re-entered the ministry as a forgiven man.

God does not forgive and then file it away for future reference; He forgives and then erases the record. The pages of transcript that record our sinning are erased clean.

Even the tape recording of our confession is erased, so that none will ever have access to our past. The guilt is removed and so is the evidence. This is the way God forgives the repentant one. Acts 3:19 urges us, "Repent ye therefore, and be converted, that your sins may be blotted out [Greek *exaleiphein*], when the times of refreshing shall come from the presence of the Lord."

Restoration

The third example of forgiveness that illustrates the process in an understandable way is the *restoring of a son*. In the fifteenth chapter of the Gospel of Luke we have the oft-told story of the prodigal son, who preferred his father's goods to his father's government. In a most demanding way, he instructed his father to divide the inheritance between the brothers while the father still lived, so that he could do whatever he pleased with his share. How easily we fall into the trap of seeing God's gifts as His debts to us. How often our prayers are as demanding of God's possessions, as though they were wages due us or loans we had made to Him. Thoughtful listening to most public prayer will reveal that we still command God to do and to give far more than we bless God and express our love to Him.

But the father graciously divided the inheritance and watched his son cash in all that had been given him and journey to "a far country" (*see* Luke 15:13). Far from God is never a matter of distance, but a matter of our affections. Satan stood as the anointed cherub that covered the mercy seat and was separated from God in his affections, while many a weak human being has found himself raptured right into the consciousness of God's presence while still confined to a human body and restricted to the earth.

The story graphically tells of the son's riotous living and how he soon had reduced himself to a level of dire poverty.

He sank so low that he hired himself out as a keeper of swine, something that was totally prohibited to a Jew, and was paid so little he wanted to eat of the swine's food just to keep from starving.

Such is the result of rebelling against the father's government and yearning to get out from under the father's eye. He was tired of the father's management and proudly declared that he could do much better, if only given the chance. But he, as have multitudes since him, found that the heavenly Father's way cannot be improved upon. Father's thrifty management seemed quite an asset when the famine came, but it had been rejected during the season of plenty. All that he had demanded from the father had long ago been used up, and he discovered that strangers can be very severe taskmasters.

In the midst of his misery, he began to remember better days and how differently his father treated the servants than he was being treated in this land, until finally he "came to himself" (*see* Luke 15:17). The madness of his chosen way of life lifted long enough for sanity to return, and in that moment, repentance began to rise within him. "I will arise and go to my father, and will say unto him, Father, I have sinned against heaven, and before thee" (Luke 15:18). He would not plead his plight—he would repent of his actions. He began to realize that he had sinned against not only his earthly father, but against God Himself.

In him, as in us, repentance was followed by conversion and "he arose, and came to his father" (*see* Luke 15:20). A change of action followed his change of attitude. There is no indication of haste on his part; more likely it was a sad, slow journey home. As painful as it would be to have to admit not only that he was wrong but that his father had been right, the prodigal had seen the lovingkindness of his father over the years and knew that he would be as well treated as the servants, and that was all he intended to request.

But long before he got to the family home, the father saw him and enthusiastically ran to him, walking the final portion of the journey with the returning son. Not only that— he warmly kissed the son and called the servants to clothe the boy with the best in the house. A ring was placed on his finger as a symbol of authority and wealth and a welcome-home party was prepared. The father sang, "This my son was dead, and is alive again; he was lost, and is found" (*see* Luke 15:24). It was a time for joy and happiness. A lost relationship had been restored.

And so it is when we finally come to ourselves and come back to the Father. Some come to themselves and never make the effort to return to the Father, but those of us who came found a warm welcome, an enthusiastic reception, a restoration of position, authority, and relationship. We returned willing to be a servant but were received as a son raised from the dead. We were not required to give an account of our behavior during the long separation, nor did He ask what had happened to all the wealth we had taken with us. He did not ask us to give an accounting, but only to accept His offer of reconciliation. He still loved us no matter what we had done and was anxious to help restore us to the better life we had known before we departed from Him.

The son left in rebellion, involved himself in riotous living, and ended in ruin, but the father soon robed, ringed, and restored the repentant son. How like God!

God's forgiveness ransoms his man, pays his debts, and restores him to sonship. David certainly experienced this, for he cried, "For thou, Lord, art good, and ready to forgive; and plenteous in mercy unto all them that call upon thee" (Psalms 86:5).

But of course there is a proportion to God's forgiveness. There is a balance and a relation of one part to another, and if we break the symmetry of divine forgiveness, we will get a distorted picture.

7

The Proportion of Forgiveness

Photography has been my hobby since my preteen days, so naturally I enjoy watching a real professional at work. When the portrait photographer sets up to take a picture, he seems never to be satisfied. He constantly adjusts the position of the lights, their intensity, the angle of the camera, the placement of the subject, and so on. He is striving for the best possible ratio between highlights and shadows, between foreground and background, and between sharp focus and soft focus. His aim is get a high-quality picture, and this requires the balance that only this ratio can supply.

In order that we might have the best possible picture of divine forgiveness, we need to do some of this same perspective balancing. Just as the photographer works with blacks and whites, with varying shades of gray in between, so the picture of forgiveness has the contrasts between what God has done for us and what we must do. All white or all black will not make a picture, and neither will seeing only the divine side of forgiveness create an understandable image any more than seeing only man's side will cause us to comprehend the subject.

There are at least four factors in man's response that decidedly affect the balance or harmony in forgiveness. The first of these, obviously, is repentance with subsequent conversion. God does not forgive without repentance, and neither does He require man to forgive until repentance is offered. Forgiveness is not automatic; it is conditional. If God did not require a change of attitude as a proviso to forgiveness, man could continue to live in sin and expect automatic forgiveness. There are some who teach this universal redemption in their overemphasis of the great grace of God, but although God's provision may include the world, His first qualification is true repentance.

Since the purpose of forgiveness is to restore man's relationship with God to the state it had before sin entered, it will require the cooperation of both parties. God alone cannot restore man to fellowship, man must desire that fellowship. There must be both a granting and an acceptance of the forgiveness. There is no question about the granting of forgiveness, for God has assured it to us in a written contract called the Bible, but there is much doubt about man's acceptance of that forgiveness. Sincere, deep-felt sorrow for the wrong which works repentance (*see* 2 Corinthians 7:10) is the condition of mind which insures the acceptance of forgiveness.

Repentance is very positive, but is generally seen as negative. Because we bring human concepts into our comprehension of divine principles, we usually think of repentance as placing us in a position of subservience, petitioning for that to which we have no right. But nothing could be further from the truth. Repentance is a glorious gift of God that enables us to avert divine judgment for our sins. It was not available to many of the characters in the Bible, for there was little provision made for man to turn from his sin and to seek pardon in the Pentateuch. The many plagues reported in Exodus and Numbers were the result of man's sin against God, for which there was no alternative but to take the punishment meted out by God. Actually, one of the first examples of repentance is seen in David's response to Nathan's parable. Because David said, "I have sinned," forgiveness was granted—"you shall not die" (*see* 2 Samuel 12:13). I am confident that the thousands upon thousands of people who faced God's judgment against sin without recourse to repentance would happily change places with any of us.

In contrast to the Pentateuch, the book of Revelation begins with Christ's pleas to six of the seven churches of Asia to repent. In each case the sin they were guilty of was stated, and God threatened judgment, but to all of them He offered renewed relationship if they would only repent. He sought to entice them to repentance through His goodness, re-expressed His undying love for them, and commended them for their love for Himself. He pointed to chastisement as His way of bringing them to repentance. But if goodness, chastisement, and our love for God won't bring us to repentance, it is hopeless, for judgment doesn't cause men to repent, as the subsequent chapters of the Revelation reveal: ". . . they gnawed their tongues for pain, And blasphemed the God of heaven because of their pains and their sores, and repented not of their deeds" (Revelation 16:10, 11).

The International Standard Bible Encyclopedia observes, "The change wrought in repentance is so deep and radical as to affect the whole spiritual nature and to involve the entire personality . . . psychology shows repentance to be profound, personal and all-pervasive." God's goal in demanding repentance before applying forgiveness is not merely to see man grovel in remorse for his sin, but to produce a change of attitude from a love of sin to a hatred for it, and from a fear of God to a love of God.

Repentance has been the backbone of every revival. The way up is down. As we fall before God in deep repentance, He lifts us up into His great forgiveness. Revival may not be so much the result of a sovereign moving of God as it is man's movement toward his sovereign God, in repentance. When God's principles are followed, God's promises are performed.

The first four Beatitudes (*see* Matthew 5:3–6) build a divine staircase upon which repentant souls may rise from the dominion of the devil into the divine Kingdom of God. The "poor in spirit" have come into a consciousness of their spiritual poverty, which has thoroughly dethroned their pride. "They that mourn" have faced a sense of personal unworthiness that has produced deep grief. "The meek" have a willingness to surrender to God in genuine humility, and "they which do hunger and thirst after righteousness" have a strong spiritual desire which has created a craving appetite for the things of God that enables them to wholly abandon sin and heartily turn to God, who alone can satisfy their deep cravings. Any way we look at it, man must change his attitudes before God will change His judgments. All life changes start with man, not with God. When "we will" then "He will."

Baptism

But there is still a second factor to be brought into balance if we are ever to enjoy forgiveness. All through the Bible, men were required to conform to certain legal or formal acts before the assurance of pardon was theirs. In the Old Testament these acts consisted of specified sacrifices that were offered, and in the New Testament it was water baptism. Over the years there has been controversy over water baptism, not only as to the method or the formula, but also as to its necessity and its meaning. To some it seems like such an empty and degrading thing to do, and to others, who have caught a glimpse of God's grace, it seems so unnecessary. Likely the same arguments were offered concerning the sacrifices for sin.

But the fact does remain that baptism was demanded by John, taught by Jesus, and practiced by Paul. Neither the Old Testament sacrifices nor the New Testament water baptism is ever seen as the meritorious grounds for forgiveness; instead, each is viewed as an outer expression of the man's inner attitude toward God. Both afforded the repentant one an opportunity to display his change of heart and mind to his friends, to himself, to spiritual principalities, and to God. They formalized and crystalized inner attitudes and created a point in experience that could be looked back upon as the beginning of a new life. His repentance and God's forgiveness were finalized by a public act very much like having a contract notarized for authenticity. Of course there can be no external substitute for an internal change, but there must be an external demonstration of that change.

Blasphemy

Still a third segment of forgiveness that must be brought into ratio to the whole is the fact that Jesus declared at least one sin to be unforgivable. All three of the synoptic Gospels record Christ's discussion of this (*see* Matthew 12:31, 32; Mark 3:28–30; Luke 12:10) and yet Satan has cleverly used this statement of Christ to convince individuals that they have committed the unpardonable sin. If we will stay with the context, there should be no difficulty in understanding what Christ was saying.

The Pharisees, who were religious rulers acquainted with the Scriptures, attributed a miraculous deed wrought by Jesus through the Spirit of God to Beelzebub. Jesus called their act blasphemy, and declared that ". . . whosoever speaketh against the Holy Ghost, it shall not be forgiven him, neither in this world, neither in the world to come" (Matthew 12:32). It is questionable if anyone could do such a thing unless his moral nature was completely warped. To such a person the distinction between good and evil would be obliterated. If he sees every act of the Holy Spirit as a work of the devil, there is no hope of winning him back. Conviction, to him, would be seen as demonic oppression. Godly sorrow would be viewed as Satanic depression. No preaching, testimony, song, or personal appeal could reach him, for he has lost all sensibilities to right and wrong. He is beyond the hope of forgiveness, not because God has set an arbitrary line of sinfulness beyond which His grace of forgiveness will not reach, but because the man has put himself beyond the possibility of arriving at the state of mind which is an essential condition to divine forgiveness. Whenever we put ourselves in a position where God's way is rejected, there remains no other way.

Throughout the years I have dealt with several who were in deep sorrow and some in heavy depression, fearing that they had committed the unpardonable sin. I assured them, upon the authority of the Word of God, that if they were even concerned about forgiveness they hadn't sinned away their day of grace. The one who has put himself in an unpardonable state has no concern, either for God or demons. His mind allows for neither. If there is sorrow for sin there is forgiveness available, no matter what the enemy may try to tell us. God has not capriciously decided that some can be saved and others must be lost; He simply says that some put themselves in a place where they cannot change their minds in repentance and no amount of grace can reach them. They are unpardonable because they are unconfessed. No repentance, no remission!

Forgiving Others

The fourth component in the human side of forgiveness that must be brought into a balanced perspective before we can identify forgiveness without distortion is the command that we forgive our fellowman who repents. On at least four occasions Jesus issued this command. In the Sermon on the Mount He said, "For if ye forgive men their trespasses, your heavenly Father will also forgive you: But if ye forgive not men their trespasses, neither will your Father forgive your trespasses" (Matthew 6:14, 15), and when He taught His disciples a model prayer, He told them to pray, "And forgive us our sins; for we also forgive every one that is indebted to us . . ." (Luke 11:4). Jesus told the story of the servant who was forgiven a debt of ten thousand talents ($7,000) because he pled for mercy and then went out and mercilessly cast a fellow servant into jail because he was unable to pay him a mere one hundred pence (about $12). He declared that the master was angry at the servant who had been forgiven so much but who had no compassion to forgive a fellow servant, and so he revoked his forgiveness and turned the poor man over to the tormentors until all ten thousand talents were paid in full. Then Jesus appended this moral to the story: "So likewise shall my heavenly Father do also unto you, if ye from your hearts forgive not every one his brother their trespasses" (Matthew 18:35).

A fourth time Jesus demanded forgiveness on the horizontal level if we are to receive it on the vertical level is in Mark 11, following His assurance that anything they desired was available to praying men. He said, "And when ye stand praying, forgive, if ye have ought against any: that your Father also which is in heaven may forgive you your trespasses" (Mark 11:25).

Patently, we must be careful, lest we see our forgiving of

a fellowman as meriting forgiveness by God. We do not trade off a forgiveness for a forgiveness. We do not earn forgiveness; it is a gift of God, and the meritorious basis is the work of Jesus at Calvary. No, our forgiving one another is not a payment to God assuring us of personal forgiveness, but it is a command that must be obeyed, and a command that has become a divine requirement for God's forgiveness.

Probably the reason Jesus so emphasized this need to forgive one another is that this act reveals the genuineness of our repentance toward God. A person who seeks forgiveness but does not forgive others hardly knows what he is asking God for and is not worthy of it. Forgiven ones make the best forgivers. If God's mercy has touched our lives, it should flow through our lives to others. If we have learned how life changing forgiveness can be, we will yearn for an opportunity to help another's life change. Jesus said, ". . . freely ye have received, freely give" (Matthew 10:8), and Peter told the lame man at gate Beautiful, ". . . such as I have give I thee . . ." (Acts 3:6). What God has given to us, He expects to be given through us to others. Forgiveness is not given merely to be received, but to be shared. Its purpose is the complete removal of all estrangement and alienation between God and man and between man and man. Forgiveness restores completely the relationship which existed prior to the sin. *The International Standard Bible Encyclopaedia* says, "God's forgiveness is conditional upon man's forgiveness of the wrongs done him, not because God forgives grudgingly but because forgiveness alone indicates that disposition of mind which will humbly accept the Divine pardon." So my forgiving my brother is as strong an indication of my attitude toward repentance as my submission to water baptism; and it is repetitive, as Peter well learned when he was told to be willing to forgive a sinning brother seventy times seven in one day (*see* Matthew 18:22).

Forgiving Ourselves

But one area in which most of us are very remiss in forgiving a fellow human being is in forgiving ourselves. I have met many people who have successfully forgiven others of grave wrongs and injustices but who have not been able to forgive themselves of far lesser offenses. When I have pressed them to believe that God has forgiven them, the response has generally been, "Yes, I honestly know that God has forgiven me, but I can't forgive myself." Sound familiar? Most of us have thought it, and many of us have actually said it. Are we suggesting that we are higher than God, and that although He has forgiven us, we are overruling Him? Have we become the supreme court of our lives? Or do we feel that God forgave us because He didn't have all of the facts at hand and made a hasty judgment?

Paul the Apostle was forgiven much and had to learn to forgive himself. I have often pondered what a difficult process this may have been for him and have wondered if this is why he was sent into the desert for the first three years after his conversion. If he hadn't learned to forgive himself, every time he was persecuted, he would have felt God was punishing him for what he had done to the Christians before his conversion. His writings would have been filled with self-pity and frightful condemnation. But Paul learned how to live like a forgiven man. He wrote, "For I am the least of the apostles, that am not meet to be called an apostle, because I persecuted the church of God. But by the grace of God I am what I am: and his grace which was bestowed upon me was not in vain; but I laboured more abundantly than they all: yet not I, but the grace of God which was with me" (1 Corinthians 15:9, 10). Instead of living in reproach or deep introspection, Paul was content to let God be the judge. He believed that God, who knew the very secrets of his heart, had judged him fairly and had forgiven him freely.

How much healthier we would be if we would follow his example. Guilt is such a destructive force in the life of a Christian that Satan does everything in his power to see to it that the guilt is not remitted toward self. He cannot stop God from forgiving us but often very successfully stops us from forgiving ourselves, and that accomplishes his purpose of destruction in the life of the believer.

A few years ago this was dramatically illustrated in my own life. In leading a growing congregation into a more vital relationship with God, I made a rather serious mistake that hurt some people very deeply. I deeply repented of this sin and was forgiven both by the individuals affected and by God. But I had difficulty forgiving myself. Well over a year later, long after the hurts were healed and the church was flowing in increasingly higher channels of worship, I joined my Sunday-school staff members in a pre-Sunday-school prayer meeting. In my early praying something triggered my memory circuits to remind me of my past failure, and I began to confess it to the Lord again. The more I repented of the thing, the greater became my sense of sorrow. Repeatedly I told the Lord that I should have known better, that my years of experience should have prevented my involvement in such a thing, and I generally berated myself before God.

Of course the more I castigated myself verbally the lower my emotions fell, until I actually put my head under the bench as I wept and sobbed before the Lord. At this point the bell rang, signaling the start of classes, but I was in no condition to teach, so I gestured to my assistant teacher to fill my place while I continued to repent of my sin.

When the room had emptied of the entire staff, I was tapped on the shoulder by the wife of one of the church's board members, who very apologetically told me that she felt the Lord had given her a word for me, but that it was to be given to me in private. Grasping for any encouragement that might be available, I urged her to share that word with me. She is a very timid person and had wrestled with the responsibility of speaking what she thought was a word from the Lord directly to her pastor until inner tension had built to the exploding point. When I finally convinced her that whatever God had given to her would be accepted without prejudice, she sat down on the bench beside me and in a voice that was heard all the way into the main sanctuary of the church she screamed, "God says, 'Shut up, you liar. There hasn't a word of truth come out of your mouth in the past thirty minutes.'"

Hearing her timid little voice screaming so frightened her that she ran out of the prayer room, down the hall, right past the ushers, and out of the building. Almost instantly two church deacons rushed into the room to see what I had done to cause this woman to cry out in such alarm and run from the church. Rather than try to explain, I insisted that they go get her and bring her back in.

She adequately explained my innocence of behavior, and after they left I asked her if that was the entire message from God.

"No," she said, "there is more, but I was so frightened I just ran."

After calming her fears somewhat, I urged her to give me the rest of what God had said in her heart.

"Judson," the message continued, "you have been confessing a nonexistent sin. Everything you have been saying is a lie, for when you genuinely confessed this thing many months ago I forgave it, cleansed it, removed all of heaven's record of it. It no longer exists, except in your memory. When you continue to confess what I have forgiven, it evidences both a weakness of faith in my forgiveness and an unwillingness to forgive yourself. When will you learn not to uncover what the blood has covered? Remember what happened when the men of Beth-shemesh lifted the mercy seat off the ark to make certain that everything was intact inside? The Lord slew over fifty thousand of them as punishment. Whenever you dare to uncover what the blood has covered, the righteous vengeance of the law will come out against you. I have forgiven you; now forgive yourself and stop talking about it.''

It was a great lesson for me, even if it had to come in an embarrassing way. Because I would not forgive myself, I had some doubts about God's forgiveness, so I was trying to reopen the case to gain new assurance. God showed me how dangerous this can be. If we have won the case, why would we want to have another trial, anyway?

Perhaps the biggest hindrance to self-forgiveness is our memory circuits. When God forgives, He forgets, but we lack the control that could erase our memories. God leaves the memories intact as a deterrent to a repeat performance, but there are a thousand little things that can trigger this circuit, and when it is activated, much of the emotion of guilt and remorse can be rekindled. But we should not respond to this false emotion, lest it drag us back into a sorrow that is not a godly sorrow. When memory reminds us of past sins, we should use it as a reminder to praise and thank the Lord for His forgiveness and to rejoice in all of the benefits of being forgiven. The more we dwell in our past failures the more we will cloud a beautiful present. We must let yesterday's failures lie buried in the sea of God's forgetfulness and grasp today as a whole new section of time and enjoy it. God has forgiven us; we must learn to forgive ourselves.

Jesus said, ". . . unless you change your whole outlook and become like little children you will never enter the kingdom of Heaven" (Matthew 18:3 PHILLIPS). One of the admirable characteristics of a child is his quickness to forgive himself. When he is wrong he accepts correction or chastisement, but once it is over he is at peace with himself and with others. He doesn't spend the next week in deep introspection; he accepts that he was wrong and has been forgiven. This quality is needed in all of our lives. We need to accept divine correction without going into dangerous introspection, and we must apply God's forgiveness to our attitudes toward ourselves.

There Is No Condemnation

But so far we've only seen the shadows. We have yet to see the highlights that form the picture. If forgiveness were entirely of man's doing, what a black void we would have on our film; but man's side merely forms the shadows that accentuate the beauty of God's side.

When a master photographer has achieved the best possible balance between dark and light, he then focuses his attention on dimensions in order to gain a pleasing symmetry of the subject. He doesn't want an angle to accentuate the length of a nose, nor will he position the hands so as to make them look disproportionate to the rest of the body. Everything must be balanced in proper harmony to attain a good portrait. Just so, we must critically view God's forgiveness with an eye to appreciate the full dimensions of His provision in ratio as well as in contrast to man's participating in that forgiveness.

The eighth chapter of Romans gives us a pleasing

perspective of divine forgiveness. It begins by saying,
"There is therefore now no condemnation to them which
are in Christ Jesus, who walk not after the flesh, but after
the Spirit" (Romans 8:1). The "now" refers back to the
final verse of chapter seven, in which Paul declared,
". . . So then with the mind I myself serve the law of
God . . . ." A change of mind, a reversal of attitude, a
repentance of heart had brought him to a place where there
was no more condemnation. And the Greek word he uses
for "no" is *oudeis,* which can be literally translated as "not
even one." We are not forgiven the big things and then held
accountable for the little things. We are not forgiven merely
the sins of the past, but the sins of the present as well. God
forgives sins of commission and of omission equally. He
forgives our unlawful desires as rapidly as He pardons our
lawless deeds. Forgiveness covers all sin; there is not even
one little condemnation left after God forgives the repentant heart. When Jesus cried "It is finished," every sin we
would ever confess was brought under this "no condemnation" clause of God's contract.

Admittedly, this doesn't seem to fit human experience.
Many a person who has zealously confessed sin and earnestly forsaken it has sensed continuing condemnation, or
so he thought. This has led many to read into the phrase "to
them which are in Christ Jesus" a meaning that was not
intended by the Holy Spirit. They have assigned this verse
in Romans 8:1 to the supersaints or to the outstandingly
spiritual ones in our churches. But this does violence to the
entire New Testament, which regularly declares all born-
again believers to be "in Christ Jesus." Verse nine of this
chapter defines this expression in saying, "But ye are not in
the flesh, but in the Spirit, if so be that the Spirit of God
dwell in you. Now if any man have not the Spirit of Christ,
he is none of his" (Romans 8:9). So verse one is not calling

for an extra conversion experience, or for an abnormally high spiritual walk in Christ Jesus. It merely states that if the Holy Spirit has placed us in Christ Jesus, there is not even one little condemnation left in God's attitude toward us.

But very likely our conflict is less theological than it is linguistic. Often we confuse condemnation with conviction or accusation, and while each deals with the law, condemnation is always associated with the penalty of the law, while accusation and conviction are concerned with our behavior toward that law.

Here in Romans 8 the Greek word we have translated as "condemnation" is *katakrima,* which means "the judgment against." When the verb form *katakrino* is used, it means "to judge down." Every New Testament use of the word *condemnation* is concerned with judgment, or the handing down of the sentence of the law.

Assume for a moment that I am a guest speaker in your city and that you have loaned me your automobile for my convenience. If you have a one-way street in the community, it is entirely possible that, as a stranger to your traffic patterns, I may drive down that street headed the wrong way, and if I did, I can assure you that a policeman would spot me quickly, for I'm very lucky that way. Signaling me to the curb with flashing lights, he would walk to my car and politely inform me that my behavior was in violation of the law of that city. There would be no point in arguing, inasmuch as my car was headed east while the arrow on the sign obviously pointed west. His accusation was just and very shortly was written on a traffic ticket which summoned me to appear in traffic court.

On the day of my appearance in court, a member of the court, whose title varies from state to state, would read the charge against me and I would be asked to enter a plea. I have the right to be represented by an attorney and can resist the accusation if I choose, for, thank God, in America we are considered innocent until proved guilty. But whether I choose to be represented or merely represent myself, I do not have to admit my guilt. However, for the sake of the illustration let's assume that I ask for a full trial and secure a lawyer for myself.

On the date of the trial my lawyer faces the accusing lawyer and pleads extenuating circumstances that had distracted me momentarily and explains to the court that as a visitor to the area I was unaware of the law.

To this the representative of the court points out that ignorance of the law is no excuse and has the arresting officer take the stand to testify that he witnessed my driving the wrong way on a one-way street.

After the arguments are heard, the court returns a verdict of guilty. At that moment I am convicted. The officer accused me, the court convicted me, but I am not yet condemned. It is not until the judge begins to read the sentence of the law that applies to my violation of the law that I come under condemnation. When he declares, "fifty dollars or thirty days in jail," I know that I have been condemned, for condemnation is always associated with the handing down of the just verdict of the law.

Now my conscience, Satan, saints, and even sinners may accuse me, but that is no more condemnation than when the officer gives out a traffic ticket. If I try to settle the financial condemnation of the law with the arresting officer, I will soon discover myself charged with attempting to bribe an officer of the law. He has no authority to hand down the condemnation of the law or to accept any settlement I may choose to offer. He can only accuse me of misbehavior; he can neither condemn nor justify me. Similarly, accusation is as far as others can go in bringing us into condemnation.

They cannot hand down the judgment of the law, for it is God's law, and only He can mete out its judgments or justify us before that law.

To help us get a broader dimension of God's forgiveness, let's use our sanctified imaginations and find ourselves hailed into heaven's court by three separate accusers.

First, let's assume that it is Satan who has lodged charges against us and who will be attempting to prosecute us. His Greek name is *Satanas,* which means "adversary or false accuser," and he is living up to that title in this suit. We know that we are innocent of the charge, but we must appear in court to answer the charges anyway. As we come before God in the august courtroom of heaven, we are nearly overcome with the majesty and awesomeness of the scene.

Our first act is to request a court-appointed lawyer because of our poverty, so God the Father appoints God the Son to represent us. Assuring us that He is already acquainted with the case and that we have nothing to worry about, we are instructed to plead "not guilty," whereupon Satan begins to bring in his evidence. Everything seems to be well documented, and he argues his case with such skill that at times we question our innocence as we see the evidence piling up. When he finally rests his case, Christ Jesus takes the stand.

"Your honor," He says to the Father, "the accuser has admitted that all of the evidence presented to this court has come from his own private investigators, his demon hordes. Aside from this, there is no evidence available. Since Satan is a proven liar, and the father of lies, and all his kingdom is built upon lies, I move that this case be thrown out of court for lack of admissible evidence."

Although Satan objects most vehemently, God the judge quickly agrees with Christ our attorney that none of the evidence is valid, since it comes from such disreputable sources.

"Case dismissed."

And we learn the beauty of "There is therefore now no condemnation to them which are in Christ Jesus . . . ."

But instead of it being Satan who hails us into court, let's assume that it is the devil, a title which comes from the Greek word *Diabolos,* which literally means "accuser or slanderer." It is a very accurate title for him, for he begins his work among men in Genesis by accusing God to man, progresses throughout the rest of the book accusing man to man, until in the book of Revelation we see him accusing man before God. In his work as *Diabolos* he functions more as a district attorney, for very likely he has the goods on us and his evidence comes from sources that will be accepted in heaven. As Satan he is harassing us without expecting to get a conviction, but as the devil he has every hope of getting a conviction against us that will condemn us eternally.

Once again heaven's court appoints Christ Jesus as our attorney, and after the case is ready for a hearing we are told to plead "not guilty."

"But, Lord," we say, "I can't do that in this courtroom, for both of us know that I am guilty."

"What we both know is that you did what you are accused of doing, but what I know is that you are legally not guilty. Now leave the handling of the law to Me and plead 'legally not guilty.' "

Realizing our total incompetence in a court of law, we do as we are told, but with great misgivings. As witness after witness is called to tell and retell our misdeed, our apprehension becomes fear. We don't have a chance. The case is airtight.

But we haven't counted on the skill of our attorney.

When it is His turn to speak in our defense, He begins to weave a pattern of violation of both the law and our rights in the collecting of the evidence that was used against us. Without ever once denying our participation in the wrongdoing, He points to search without warrant, arrest without disclosure of our rights, and various and sundry other improprieties in the building of the case against us.

"Your honor," Christ Jesus says, "I move for an acquittal in this case."

Before the devil can fully recover himself, God has ruled "not guilty; case closed."

"There is therefore now no condemnation to them who are in Christ Jesus . . . ."

I had an occasion to see this in action several years ago, when I was pastoring. A very fine young man in our congregation was just months away from his high-school graduation with plans to enter Bible school in training for the ministry. One Sunday afternoon some of his fellow students prodded him into borrowing his father's pickup truck and driving them to the coast to pick up some things they had over there. Enroute home he learned that the items were stolen goods, and he realized that he was now an accessory to the crime. The companions were thrilled to have their "goody boy" involved with them in crime.

Perhaps through carelessness or perhaps as a show of bravado, this young man began to drive faster and faster, until he was pulled over to the side by a state patrolman who became suspicious when he saw what was in the bed of the pickup and took some of the goods from the truck to his own car. A later check proved that the items were stolen, and all of the young fellows were arrested.

The parents of the driver were heartbroken, for they feared a conviction would keep him from entering the ministry. The young man was overcome with remorse and

sorrow and even refused the services of the attorney his
father engaged. Finally the father and I persuaded him to
put himself in the hands of this attorney and to follow his
advice in pleading "legally not guilty." It took a lot of talking to show him the difference between being guilty of a
misdeed and being guilty in the eyes of the law.

Showing the court that the goods used in evidence against
the young man had been seized without a warrant, the
lawyer succeeded not only in having the case dismissed but
in having the arrest and jail records obliterated so that today
it is impossible to find any written record against this young
man, although he spent nearly a week in the county jail.

Never will Satan (the false accuser) or the devil (the true
accuser) win a case against the person who genuinely repented of his sin before court begins its session. Christ
Jesus will always get the repentant one off without condemnation.

But Lucifer (his true name, for Satan and devil are really
titles) is not the only one who can accuse us before God.
Sometimes it is a fellow believer that hails us into court.
Remember how God told Cain that the blood of his brother
Abel ". . . crieth unto me from the ground" (Genesis
4:10)? Prayers of complaint register charges against us that
will not go unnoticed. My wrong to a fellow believer must
be righted, or God will take vengeance on me. Even my
sinning against a nonbeliever is answerable before God.

Assume with me that I have been hailed into heaven's
court by the complaint of someone here on earth. The case
against me is quite obvious, and I don't have any plea to
make except "guilty as charged." There are no clever legal
maneuvers that will let me off this time. The brother's case
is just, and I am guilty.

Imagine my surprise when Christ Jesus pleads double

jeopardy on my behalf. He explains that I cannot be tried for a crime for which I have already been convicted of and have paid the penalty.

"But when was he convicted of this crime?" the judge asks.

"In A.D. 32 in Jerusalem, your honor," my attorney replies.

Turning to the prosecuting attorney, God asks, "And when was it you said this sin was committed?"

"In 1978, your honor. I don't see how the plea of double jeopardy can apply here."

"Let me explain," Christ says. "Right after the defendant was made aware of his sin, he fully repented of that sin and confessed it to Me. By faith he projected that sin to My cross at Calvary and accepted the divine judgment that was meted out upon Me that dark afternoon as the judgment that is due him. He received My condemnation as though it were his, just as I received his as though it were Mine. That is why I say that this man, whose offense was not actually carried out until 1978, actually paid the full penalty for it in A.D. 32."

"Case dismissed," the judge declares. "No man can be convicted twice of the same sin. Since the penalty has already been paid, there can be no condemnation at this time."

When we focus our attention on God's side of forgiveness, we are assured that there will never be condemnation handed down against any person who has sincerely and scripturally repented.

Paul pens it rather poetically when he writes, "Who shall lay any thing to the charge of God's elect? It is God that justifieth. Who is he that condemneth? It is Christ that died, yea rather, that is risen again, who is even at the right hand of God, who also maketh intercession for us'' (Romans 8:33, 34).

Because of Christ we need not fear God's judgments, for He will always apply the righteousness of the law, not its condemnation. God is satisfied once we have repented and exacts no further penalty.

This pattern of complete forgiveness is seen from one end of the Bible to the other and is illustrated in a great variety of ways, but all of them are part of God's great pattern of forgiveness.

8

The Pattern of Forgiveness

There are three Hebrew words and three Greek words used in the Bible which the King James Version translates as "forgive," and they illuminate three shades of meaning from "to cover," to "let go," to "lift up or carry away." All of these words convey the idea that when God forgives man there is a separating of that man from his sins and while the man is brought into a nearness with God, the sins are put away. Forgiveness removes the sin from the sinner, destroys that sin, and then regenerates the man.

Because God knows how much easier it is for man to think in concrete rather than abstract ideas, God has given us several explicit illustrations of forgiveness in picture language throughout the Old Testament. Three of them will suffice to picture what these words for forgiveness are trying to convey. Each of them is a divine provision of God to handle the eruption of sin. While they are only shadows, they do prove the existence of true substance and illustrate how great that substance really is.

If God ever revealed Himself to be a redeemer, it was to Israel in delivering her from three hundred years of slavery down in Egypt. God provided them a deliverer in the person of Moses, although they weren't asking to be delivered, and with great grace and mighty signs and wonders God forced their release. From the opening of the Red Sea, with its subsequent closing upon their enemies, to the provision of water and manna, plus the divine guidance in the pillar of fire and the cloud, God showed His providential care and His paternal love for them. It was truly a redeeming love that lifted them from the status of slavery and established them as God's chosen people.

But when God got this people to Mount Sinai and began to offer a personal relationship to them, it so overwhelmed them that they rejected it totally. Deuteronomy 5 tells the story to the second generation. They preferred law to relationship and offered to do anything God wanted done but refused to be what He wanted them to be: "a kingdom of priests" (*see* Exodus 19:6). They refused to listen to the voice of the Lord; they feared a personal relationship with God, and insisted that they would die if God ever spoke to them again. They offered Moses and their elders to God as a substitute. Just as we do, they ". . . turned every one to his own way . . ." (Isaiah 53:6) and in doing so committed the primeval sin, that of rejecting God's rule and authority.

God told Moses that whether the people wanted Him or not, He intended to remain in the camp and would provide a means whereby sinful man could approach a holy God. That means was the Tabernacle. It was both God's residence among men and man's avenue of approach to God. In its every detail it pictures Jesus Christ. In my book *Let Us Draw Near* I examine each portion of the Tabernacle with a view of seeing another facet of this lovely God-man who came to earth to become man's means of approach to God.

Suffice it here to say that God chose the entire tribe of Levi to become priests unto God in the place of Israel, who had refused the office. God's Tabernacle and priesthood were to become the means whereby man could rid himself of his sin and God could satisfactorily atone those sins, thereby making relationship with Himself possible once again. Sin had to be covered or put out of sight, and that is exactly what the Hebrew word *kaphar* means, although we have translated it as "forgive." God's provision, through the rituals surrounding the Tabernacle, caused their sins to loose away or be loosed from them. That is the true meaning of the Greek word *apoluo,* which we also translate as "forgive."

The first of these rituals that provided a covering for sin was the shedding and sprinkling of blood at the brazen altar. Leviticus 17:11 declares, "For the life of the flesh is in the blood: and I have given it to you upon the altar to make an atonement for your souls: for it is the blood that maketh an atonement for the soul." Here the word *kaphar,* "covering," is used. In referring to this, Hebrews declares, "And almost all things are by the law purged with blood; and without shedding of blood is no remission" (Hebrews 9:22). So "covering" (or "atonement") and "remission" are seen as the same thing, and both came by virtue of the giving of the life of an innocent victim through this shedding of blood.

This shedding of blood to make an atonement was so much a part of the Tabernacle worship as to cause some critics to call it a "butcher religion." It is not a pleasant scene, but there is nothing pleasant about cleaning up sin. Sin is a mess, and removing it is messy, too. We know, of course, that the blood answers to the penalty of sin. It is substitutionary atonement; that is, an innocent dies for the guilty, thereby satisfying the penalty of the law. The priests had to make atonement for themselves with blood, and they spent most of their daylight hours making a blood atonement for the sins of the people. But once the penitent laid his hands upon the victim's head and confessed his sins, he accepted, by faith, that the sins that were once his had now become the animal's, so that when the life of the animal was drawn out and sprinkled on the man, he believed that he was released from the penalty and had been given a new life—the life that was sprinkled upon him in the type of the blood. He was "covered," atoned. His debt had been paid in full, howbeit it was done by another on his behalf.

This is what Jesus has done for us at Calvary. He loosed us from our sin and covered that sin's penalty in His own death.

A second Tabernacle ritual that speaks of loosing away our sins is the laver, which was a large water-filled basin made of the bronze mirrors that the women had donated. The priests were commanded to wash their faces, hands, and feet every time they went into the holy place to minister at the candlestick, the table of shewbread, or the golden altar, and they had to wash again as they came out of that holy place. The meaning was obvious; in their ministering on behalf of the sins of the people, the priests got dirty. They were not to approach a holy God in a defiled condition; they were to pause, inspect, and cleanse themselves before coming in.

The picture of water loosing the defilement and flushing it away onto the desert sands is an apt picture of God loosing us from our sins by the "washing of the water of the word" (*see* Ephesians 5:26). As we embrace and apply, by faith, the promises of God's Word, we are cleansed from the defilements and stain of sin. The blood answers the penalty of sin, but the Word handles the pollution of sin. It is not sufficient for a man's sins to be covered by the blood; he needs to be cleansed by the water of the Spirit and the Word.

For the high priest who came all the way into the presence of God on the day of atonement, there was still a third ritual in which to involve himself. In addition to the blood and the water, he was completely stripped of all the garments he wore in the outer court and was clothed with pure white linen garments which were only worn in God's presence. Whereas the blood answered the penalty of sin and the water cleansed the pollution of sin, this stripping totally removed the presence of sin, and he was clothed with special garments which are defined in the book of Revelation as ". . . the righteousness of saints" (Revelation 19:8). The blood settles man's position before God, the water alters man's condition in life, and the change of garments makes possible a transition from service to man to ministry unto the Lord.

Sin is covered, put out of sight, and loosed away. That is a beginning picture of divine forgiveness as given to us in the Tabernacle.

A second pattern of forgiveness that was given to Israel as a visual aid to understanding the removal of sin was the scapegoat. Leviticus 16 records God's commandments about this unusual ceremony that was part of the preparation for the high priest to enter the Holy of Holies on the day of atonement. For sinful man to come directly into the presence of a Holy God was an awesome experience that required much preparation, including the shedding and sprinkling of the blood of a sacrifice; thorough washing with water; fire and incense in the portable censer; a complete stripping of the high priest and reclothing him with the pure white linen; plus this unusual ceremony of the scapegoat.

This ceremony began by selecting two goats to be offered as a sin offering. Lots were cast to determine which was to be for the Lord and which was to be for Azaziel (the word we have translated as "scapegoat"). The first goat was slain as a sin sacrifice; "But the goat, on which the lot fell to be the scapegoat, shall be presented alive before the Lord, to make an atonement with him, and to let him go for a scapegoat into the wilderness'' (Leviticus 16:10). Before this goat was released, however, Aaron (and in subsequent generations, the high priest) was commanded to ''. . . lay both his hands upon the head of the live goat, and confess over him all the iniquities of the children of Israel, and all their transgressions in all their sins, putting them upon the head of the goat, and shall send him away by the hand of a fit man into the wilderness'' (Leviticus 16:21).

Scholars have had some difficulty with this one goat being assigned to Azaziel, but most of them agree that this was a symbolic act intended to assure Israel that her sins had been removed from the camp forever. *The Zondervan Pictorial Bible Encyclopedia* says, ''. . . in all likelihood this custom meant no more than a symbolic transfer of sin from the realm of society into that of death.'' *The New Standard Bible Dictionary* says, ''In Israel it . . . was used to express the thought that sin belongs to a power or principle hostile to Jehovah and its complete purgation must include its being sent back to its source.''

When we realize that the scapegoat was only one segment of a two-part sacrifice for sin, we realize also that Christ's death had two functions in it for the believer. Through the death of the first goat, atonement was made; the sin account was settled. But through the laying of the sin upon the second goat and leading him into an uninhabited place, indicating the absolute impossibility of its return, Israel was assured that the guilt was forever removed from the camp in general and their lives in particular.

Christ came not only to settle the account of sin but to remove the guilt of sin from the lives of believers. It is not enough to have the record clear; we need our consciences clear as well, for even if we are not guilty in the eyes of the law, as long as we are guilty in our own eyes we live in misery.

Yesterday there was a story on the front page of the *Dallas Times Herald* that powerfully illustrates this principle. It had a dateline of Poland and told of a man who had just been discovered hiding in the attic of his sister's barn. He had been active with the Nazis during World War II and at the end of the war had hidden himself, fearing reprisals of the law. During all of these years he had seen no one but his sister, had been cut off from all contact with the outside world, subsisting on what little food his sister would bring him, and had limited his activities to the small room in the attic. When the authorities found him, they checked their records and told him that there had never been any charges against him. They have never wanted him for anything.

He had been a totally free man, as far as the law was concerned, but had been in a self-imposed imprisonment for thirty or so years because of unremitted guilt. As I read it, I thought of wasted years in my life because I refused to believe that Christ was not only my sin sacrifice but was also my scapegoat, who had removed all of my guilt so far from me that it could never return.

This principle of guilt's removal is suggested in two of the words we have translated "forgive" in our Bible. The Hebrew word *salach* literally means "to let go; send away" while the Greek word *aphiemi* means "to send off or away." So in both Testaments we have a word that means what this demonstration has just shown; that God has provided an answer to not only the penalty of sin but to its presence as well. Sin is removed from us, borne away to an uninhabited place. Since sin had a source, it is fitting that when it is removed from our life it be returned to that source. We don't want it around as a living souvenir of past miseries; we want every vestige of it removed, so that even our memories will have a chance to forget the days that we walked in our own way. The scapegoat is outside of the camp forever. Hallelujah!

But there is still a third Old Testament pattern of forgiveness that illuminates another aspect of God's pardoning grace. It is the occurrence that Jesus likened Himself to when He said, ". . . as Moses lifted up the serpent in the wilderness, even so must the Son of man be lifted up: That whosoever believeth in him should not perish, but have eternal life" (John 3:14, 15). Christ is, of course, referring to the incident in the wilderness as recorded in Numbers 21. Israel had murmured against God and against Moses for the fourteenth time. They were tired of the way, tired of the manna, and malcontent with just about everything. On each preceding occasion of murmuring, God had severely judged the people, but they didn't seem to learn much from this divine chastisement, so this time ". . . the Lord sent fiery serpents among the people, and they bit the people; and much people of Israel died" (Numbers 21:6). It was a fitting punishment, for murmuring always produces poison, so God merely put the poison in a visible form to let the people see immediately the consequences of discontent with the provisions and promises of God.

This time the people responded to God's chastisement differently than in their previous murmurings. "Therefore the people came to Moses, and said, We have sinned, for we have spoken against the Lord, and against thee; pray unto the Lord, that he take away the serpents from us . . ." (Numbers 21:7). They finally got around to repenting. How long it takes to learn to repent. But the moment they repented, God made a provision for the removal of the judgment. He instructed Moses to make a replica of the serpents out of brass and to put it on a pole in the midst of the camp. Any who would come to look at it would be healed of the effects of the poison (*see* Numbers 21:8).

The Zondervan Pictorial Bible Encyclopedia suggests,

"Perhaps for the first time in Biblical history the sinner's punishment could be averted, simply by looking with no suffering involved." In making the symbol of brass (actually bronze) it took on the typology of judgment, and by making it in the form of the very thing that was cursing them, it became a pictorial graphic of Christ actually being made sin for us, enduring the judgment of God against sin on a pole (cross) in the midst of His people. "Look and live" has been the theme of the Gospel ever since the death of Jesus Christ.

The Hebrew word *nasa*, which literally means "to lift up," is translated "forgive" at least sixteen times in the King James Version of the Bible. What a picture of the lifting up of the serpent and of the greater lifting up of Jesus Christ at Calvary. But the Greek word that best pictures the incident of the brazen serpent is *charizomai*, which means "to be gracious unto." To a people who had never experienced forgiveness and remission of sin as a result of repentance, this "look and live" was certainly a gracious act. All forgiveness is an act of grace, and it is God's desire to *charizomai* His children. He gains no pleasure out of judging us; He wants to fellowship us, not flog us. He desires to pardon us, not punish us. When Moses asked to see the glory of the Lord, God said, ". . . I will make all my goodness pass before thee, and I will proclaim the name of the Lord before thee; and will be gracious to whom I will be gracious, and will shew mercy on whom I will shew mercy" (Exodus 33:19). This was stated as part of the revelation of the glory of the Lord. Moses, as many since him, may have felt that God was saying it was a matter of sovereign choice as to whom God would be merciful, but the incident of the brazen serpent taught him that God would always be gracious to those who could wholeheartedly confess, "we have sinned."

These three Old Testament patterns of forgiveness give shadowy evidence that the true substance exists. The reality, of which these types could foretell only in partiality, is, of course, Christ Jesus, who came ". . . full of grace and truth" (John 1:14). He tabernacled among us (John 1:14 literal Greek), He became our Azaziel (scapegoat), bearing our guilts away forever, and He Himself declared that He was the serpent in the wilderness. He came to "cover, to loose away, to let go, to be sent away, to be lifted up, and to be gracious unto us." Everything that the Old Testament promised, He performed.

The details of the arrest, trial, and crucifixion fulfill, even to the exact hour, all of these Old Testament patterns of a vicarious, substitutionary, sacrificial lamb. He was both the High Priest and the dying Lamb. He was both the goat that was slain unto Jehovah and the goat that was released unto Azaziel. He was, in one action, the provider of the brass serpent and that serpent itself. In every facet of redemption, He is the redeemer.

In the rugged cross of Christ, we see God's supreme wisdom manifested in being able to love the sinner and yet hate his sin; in remaining totally just while being an available justifier of all who would seek Him. God's plan enabled Him to destroy sin while giving life to the sinner. The cross was and is God's total answer to Satan, to the power of sin, to the penalty of sin, to the presence of sin, and to the guilt of sin. By allowing us to identify with that cross, it can in one act be the end of our self-life and the beginning of His life within ourselves. Both the objective and the subjective power of the cross were released when Jesus said, "It is finished" (*see* John 19:30); that is, God was satisfied and man was saved; Satan was crushed and man was cured; sin was removed and life was restored. The negatives were canceled out and the positives were supplied.

But there is one further aspect of the work of Christ on the cross that is worth considering. Although Christ twice declared that He came to give His life "a ransom" (Greek *lutron*), when Paul says in 1 Timothy 2:6 that Christ Jesus gave himself "a ransom" for all, he uses the Greek word *antilutron*. This, I understand, is a very rare word. William Barclay declares in *New Testament Words* that it is used in Orphic literature to mean an "antidote" and "remedy." Paul seems to be saying that Christ's death has become the "antidote" for the poison of sin and the "remedy" for the infirmity of sin. We are not only delivered from sin; we can be inoculated, vaccinated, given an antidote to it, so that we can live above its effects. So great is God's forgiveness that He not only removes the penalty of past sin but has provided a preventive to future involvement in sin. He handles the past, the present, and the future all in one provision—Christ's atoning death.

9

The Purpose of Forgiveness

Just as God's provision of forgiveness is multiple, so is the purpose of forgiveness. Actually, we will probably have to await our entrance into heaven to fully understand why God forgave us of all our sins, but there are at least four distinct purposes that are revealed to us in God's Word.

The most obvious of these is to induce change in our lives. Our repentance makes conversion, "about-face," possible. When we will do what we can do, God will do what we cannot do. We cannot change our lives; God cannot repent. All of our sorrow for sin cannot prevent our reinvolvement in sin, but, as we have just seen, God's provision for forgiveness also gives us the antidote for sin.

Because of sin, our lives suffered a broken purity; we lost our innocence, just as Adam and Eve lost theirs through sin. The vacuum produced by this loss of purity was soon filled by the introduction of guilt, and that guilt forced radical changes in our lives. Whereas man was made to enjoy life, guilt caused him to endure it. Life cannot be savored by the guilty. Guilt drives a man mercilessly, and the harder he runs, the more relentlessly he is pursued. Nothing he can do will atone for the sin or remove the guilt, and much that he does only temporarily distracts his attention from the guilt or represses it chemically; but those acts only increase his guilt load later. Guilt is a dangerous force that ruins far more lives than cancer, and none of us is immune to it unless we are also immune to sin, for sin and guilt go together "like a horse and carriage."

God did not want man to live his short span of years in constant guilt, haunted by fears of reprisal or of uncontrollable power forcing a repetition of the very acts that produced the guilt in the first place. God made man to be free from guilt in order that he might enjoy his God. Divine forgiveness is God's way of restoring man to his lost innocence and purity. In being born again, man begins anew. The slate is wiped clean, and he can start over. Phillips translates 2 Corinthians 5:16, "For if a man is in Christ he becomes a new person altogether—the past is finished and gone, everything has become fresh and new" and then adds, "All this is God's doing . . ." (verse 17).

A few years ago a dozen of the pastors in a western city were invited to take a special course on counseling sponsored by the University of Oregon. I was one of the pastors invited to participate. Each week a different guest lecturer shared with us pastors, and I believe we all found it to be a beneficial morning. On the week that the subject was "How to deal with guilt," I was especially expectant; but not for long, for the lecture seemed to suggest that we can only change a person's attitude about what they have done. In effect we were being encouraged to counsel the guilty person to lower his standards to fit his behavior, so that he could walk out from under his guilt load.

I kept my mouth shut, but I couldn't totally control my body language. As the lecture ended and the discussion period began, I was asked if I had anything to say.

"No, sir," I answered very firmly.

As pastor after pastor shared his inability to handle the guilt that was brought to him in his counseling chamber, my discomfort became so apparent that the visiting psychologist looked closely at my name tag and then said, "Reverend Cornwall, it is obvious by your attitude that you disagree with what has been said so far. Suppose you tell us how you handle guilt at your church."

His straightforward challenge opened the sluice gates of the dam of my timidity, and the words poured out like floodwaters. I spoke of remission, of atonement, of vicarious death and of entering into Christ's complete victory. I told them that our church operated homes for unwed mothers, and that we had successfully brought each of these teenagers through to Christ and many of them into a fulfilled life without guilt. I probably spoke less than ten minutes, but I certainly said a lot.

When I stopped, the chairman said, "I think we had better exchange places for the rest of the morning. You be the teacher, and I'll take the course under you."

Thinking that he was mocking me, I apologized, but the pastors took up his plea, declaring that they had never heard anything like this in all of their lives and that they were vitally interested in the concept that guilt can actually be removed.

The rest of the morning was mine, and what a joy it was to show from the Scriptures, as well as to document from experience, that God's purpose of forgiveness was to remove guilt, not to lower our standards to accept that guilt.

While there are many things about myself that I must accept without any hope of change, guilt is not one of them, praise the Lord. Christ did not come to make me taller or shorter or to change the color of my eyes or the length of my nose; but He did come and die to totally deliver me from guilt so that I can enjoy a changed life—the life of a little child, the life of a sinless saint.

A second purpose for God's forgiveness of sin and sinners is to bring us out of a siege mentality: to release us not only from the prison of sin but from the prison mentality. Romans 6:14 declares, "For sin shall not have dominion over you . . . ." When we learn how to accept God's complete forgiveness, we get out of the fort and into the fray. We stop retreating from life and begin to get involved in it. How many Christians live in the fear that if they get too close to a sinner he might infect them? Their concept of maintaining holiness is to join a monastery, at least figuratively. But God's forgiveness so immunizes a man against sin that he no longers worries about "catching" it; he has become a "carrier" of righteousness and expects to infect others with it.

I lived for many years with a siege mentality. When the Lord began to beckon me out into His glorious freedom, I was far too fearful to venture out of my protective custody. During this period of God's dealing with me I had a repeated vision every morning in the prayer room. I saw myself in a jail cell in a long block of other cells. Each morning the Lord would come, unlock and open the door, and urge me to walk out to freedom. He assured me that there was no reason for me to remain in prison any longer. Each day I would venture out into the hallway a few steps, and immediately other prisoners would warn me that it was a trap. When their voices died down I could hear the roaring of lions, and I feared that at the end of this long hall the open doorway led directly into an arena filled with hungry lions. In terror I would return to my cell and close my own door.

I had fixed my cell up quite comfortably. The floor was carpeted, the windows had curtains, and all the furniture was upholstered. I had fluorescent lighting, books, and good music to help me while away my time. I was not suffering, but I was not free, nor was I of any use to God or man, living in my private cell "protected from the enemy."

On Friday of this week, just as I again had this vision of being in my jail cell, a dear saint in the prayer room put her hand on my shoulder and said, "I feel that the Lord wants me to tell you that this is the last time he'll ever ask you to step out into freedom." This meant that today's decision would be a lifetime decision. I waited for Christ to come and open my cell door, but instead He merely spoke to me from down the hall and told me that the door was unlocked and I could walk out any time I was ready.

Words cannot describe the inner trauma of the next few moments. I opened the door and took a few cautious steps down the hall, but the roaring of the lions was unmistakable. I was going to be a martyr, but I lacked martyr's grace. So I retreated back into my cell and sat on my comfortable cot. But freedom sounded wonderful, and today's decision would affect the rest of my natural life, so once again I tried to summon sufficient courage to walk out of the cell and the prison. But I couldn't do it. Every time I heard those lions, fear gripped me as an overwhelming power and drove me back into my cell.

"God, I can't do it. Help me," I cried.

"Come on out; the door is open," He answered.

This time I walked out at a fast pace, and about ten feet from my cell I heard my cell door slam shut and lock. It was unmistakable, for I had listened to that door being locked for years. I panicked, for now I couldn't retreat; there was no place to go. But God calmed me with deep assurances that I would enjoy freedom.

As I walked down the long corridor, past the cells of hundreds of other captives of fear, their voices rang out in pleadings that I not sacrifice my life to the lions. Even as I write, many years later, I can hear their mournful voices echoing and re-echoing down the concrete hallway. I held my head high and tried to act as if I was brave, but the closer I got to the light at the end of the passageway, the louder the roar of the lions became, until I fancied that I could smell their pungent odor. By now my motion seemed to be assisted by a gentle push behind me, and I sensed that I had passed the point of no return. When I got to the door I closed my eyes, and as I stepped across the threshold I expected to drop directly into a den of lions. Instead, I found myself on firm footing, completely unharmed but almost in pain for the intensity of the roaring of the lions.

Slowly I opened my eyes, and what I saw so infuriated me that I have never lost my anger for the devil since. There were no lions—only two gigantic speakers hooked up to a powerful amplifier and a tape recorder. I had been held captive by a fear of a nonexistent force, a lie! A simple tape recording had induced sufficient fear in me as to create a siege mentality, and I had voluntarily remained in my self-imposed exile when I could have been enjoying the excitement of freedom.

God sent us forgiveness in the person of His Son, Jesus, in order to remove false fears and to instill the mentality of free men in His forgiven ones.

Shortly after this experience I was introduced to a chorus that has been my victory song ever since: "I'm free from the fears of tomorrow—I'm free from the guilt of the past. I've traded my shackles for a glorious crown. I'm free, praise the Lord, free at last."

As glorious as changed lives and release from a siege mentality are, there are two even greater purposes for God's forgiveness. One is that we might be holy, blameless, sons of God. This is mentioned repeatedly in the New Testament by both Paul and Peter. Paul wrote, "Who shall also confirm you unto the end, that ye may be blameless in the day of our Lord Jesus Christ" (1 Corinthians 1:8); and "That ye may be blameless and harmless, the sons of God, without rebuke, in the midst of a crooked and perverse nation, among whom ye whine as lights in the world" (Philippians 2:15); while Peter said, "Wherefore, beloved, seeing that ye look for such things, be diligent that ye may be found of him in peace, without spot, and blameless" (2 Peter 3:14).

Blameless! Forgiven so we can be "without spot, and blameless." What consideration, what compassion, what a provision!

But after a deed has been done, even though we may be forgiven of it, how could we ever be declared blameless? We need only to remember two principles to understand this truth. First, after we are forgiven we are declared to be "sons of God." Conversion changes our relationship not only to others and to ourselves, but to our God. We who were once "sinners" are given the power to become sons of God (*see* John 1:12). This makes us recipients of the benefit of the second principle: parents bear the legal blame for their children's wrong.

My daughters were never particularly coordinated at playing baseball, but they enjoyed trying. The next-door neighbor had a lovely backyard, and my girls enjoyed playing there with their daughter. I had warned them against playing baseball in that yard, because of a particularly vulnerable window looking into the neighbor's dining room, but Daddy's instructions were easily forgotten in the excitement of play.

One late afternoon my front doorbell rang just moments after my daughters had entered the house through the back door and had rushed upstairs to their rooms. There on my front porch stood a large man with a baseball in one hand

and a broken piece of glass in the other. He really didn't need to explain what had happened. His face told the story.

He did not ask to see my daughters, nor did he issue any threats against them. He merely wanted to know how rapidly I was going to be able to replace the broken window. You see, he and I knew that although the deed had been committed by my children, the blame was mine, not theirs. They were minors and I was legally responsible for all of their mistakes. I apologized for their behavior and replaced the window that very afternoon.

Since we have become God's children, He has accepted, by virtue of being our Father, the legal responsibility for the blame of our behavior. Once He has settled the accounts, He may very well chasten us to discourage a repetition of the act, just as I did with my girls, but the blame is still His. He must fix the window, or whatever.

This, of course, is not intended to give us license to do wrong, any more than God's grace is a license to sin. But it does serve to protect us from satanic charges against our behavior. Because we are minors, God says that He will do the correcting, and Satan is to file all charges directly to the Father and to leave the children alone. No, none of God's goodness is to be misused. Several times Jesus urged forgiven ones to "go and sin no more," and this is the theme of the epistles. As I have said in my book *Let Us Be Holy,* "God is for man, but not as a sinner; only as a potential saint." By God's bearing responsibility for our actions and accepting our blame, we are freed from past mistakes so that we can invest our energies and spiritual resources to "live godly in Christ Jesus" (*see* 2 Timothy 3:12). In his letter to Titus, Paul wrote, "For the grace of God that bringeth salvation hath appeared to all men, Teaching us that, denying ungodliness and worldly lusts, we should live soberly, righteously, and godly, in this present world"

(Titus 2:11, 12). Christ bore the guilt of our sin, the Father accepts the blame for it, and we are freed from it but stand in the likelihood of severe chastisement from God if we continue to play around in it any longer. We are blameless, but we are responsible to God for our actions. No power on earth or in hell has a right to accuse us of blame, for God's forgiveness has accepted even this by-product of sin.

But as vital, valuable, and viable as these reasons for forgiveness are, by far the greatest purpose of forgiveness is that it fulfills God's nature and satisfies His glory.

When the Israelites revolted at going into the promised land because of the unfavorable report of the ten spies, God told Moses, "I will smite them with the pestilence, and disinherit them, and will make of thee a greater nation and mightier than they" (Numbers 14:12). In Moses' intercession on behalf of the people, he pleaded God's reputation, not man's great need. He appealed to the basic goodness of God's nature and pleaded with Him that His character not be sullied in the eyes of the Egyptians by killing off the very people He had led out. "And the Lord said, I have pardoned according to thy word: But as truly as I live, all the earth shall be filled with the glory of the Lord" (Numbers 14:20, 21). God pardoned for His own sake and said that His glory would fill the earth in spite of sinning man.

In that occasion, as in our case, God's justice would warrant His rejecting, disowning, and punishing the sinner; but His love prompts Him to forgive.

Similarly, when David pled for forgiveness for his uncovered sin he prayed, "For thy name's sake, O Lord, pardon mine iniquity; for it is great" (Psalms 25:11). He did not plead his kingly position, his past greatness, or his urgent need. He pleaded for pardon for God's sake. In his knowledge of God, he seemed to have learned that it is in the very nature of God to love the sinner and to pardon his sin.

David asked God to "be himself" and thereby fulfill His nature and His glory.

Daniel prayed similarly when he supplicated, "O Lord, hear; O Lord, forgive; O Lord, give heed and act; delay not, for thy own sake, O my God, because thy city and thy people are called by thy name" (Daniel 9:19 RSV). He, too, expected God to find the highest reason for His forgiveness within Himself.

The weeping prophet Jeremiah cried out, "It is of the Lord's mercies that we are not consumed, because his compassions fail not. They are new every morning: great is thy faithfulness" (Lamentations 3:22, 23).

Judgment is not averted because we repent, but *when* we repent. Our repentance is never the grounds for or the mediacy of our forgiveness; it is merely a precondition that releases God from having to function as a judge and allows Him to flow in His genuine loving nature. We are always forgiven, because that is the very nature of God. He forgives for the same reason that a man eats: it is essential to His nature.

So we can say that the highest purpose of forgiveness is to allow God to manifest His lovingkindness and tender mercies and thereby declare, demonstrate, and dispense His glory among men.

10

The Perpetuity of Forgiveness

Since forgiveness is a manifestation of the essential nature of the Godhead and is a means whereby His glory is shown to mankind; and since the prophets have declared that "the earth shall be filled with knowledge of the glory of the Lord, as the waters cover the sea" (*see* Habakkuk 2:14; Isaiah 11:9); we would expect that God's forgiveness would increase, not decrease, as the world's population explodes and man's participation in sin expands. Although modern technology has vastly expanded the methods by which man may express his sinful nature, and today's mores give license for all to do what once was reserved for people of wealth and power, none of this caught God unaware; He was prepared. He has assured us, ". . . where sin abounded, grace did much more abound: That as sin hath reigned unto death, even so might grace reign through righteousness unto eternal life by Jesus Christ our Lord" (Romans 5:20, 21). No matter the extent of man's depravity, God's glory shall be revealed in this old world, and divine forgiveness is one of the early forms of that demonstration.

There is an unlimited periphery in God's forgiveness, as

seen first of all in His plan to forgive the entire world. God's forgiveness is available not only to the Christian, or to those of us blessed by God to have been raised in a Christian nation, but, "For God so loved the world, that he gave his only begotten Son . . ." (John 3:16). Wherever there is sin, there is need for forgiveness, and wherever there is repentance for that sin, there is forgiveness available. God has put no limits on the amount of sin He will forgive and has not established boundaries beyond which His love will extend. The greater the sin, the greater the grace; assuming repentance, of course.

But there is another sense in which there is an unlimited periphery, or boundary, in forgiveness, and that involves what God does with our confessed sins. The human concept of "I will forgive, but I can never forget" must never be applied to God's forgiveness, for as we have seen, God is not merely letting us get by with a transgression without paying a penalty; He has entered the scene of our sin and has dealt directly with both the deed and the desire. Several of the Old Testament writers, to whom we generally refer as "living under the law," caught a more-perfect vision of the extent of God's forgiveness than many of us who live "under grace."

For example, look at the book that may well date back into the days of Moses and hear Job remind God, "My transgression is sealed up in a bag, and thou sewest up mine iniquity" (Job 14:17). He does not use *sealed* in the sense of being preserved, but in the significance of being contained and concealed.

God does not hang our confessed sins out for public display like so much dirty laundry; He seals them up so that none can get a look at them. So unlike the court cases that expose all the details of our behavior to the prying eyes of the media, God chooses to gather up our confessed sins very much as nuclear wastes are sealed in drums and double sealed in concrete before being buried. Not only does this keep prying eyes out of our business, but it prevents that sin from getting back to us. Exoneration, not exposure, is God's goal for those who love Him.

David caught an even broader picture of the limitlessness of God's disposal of our sins when he sang, "As far as the east is from the west, so far hath he removed our transgressions from us" (Psalms 103:12). This is the poet's way of describing infinity. It is endless, immeasurable, and continuous.

Frequently, in dealing with repentant ones, I have been told, "I accept that God has forgiven me of my sins, but I have a great fear that I will fall back into them."

Fall back into the sins that God has forgiven? How can a person locate what God has contained, concealed, and removed into infinity? God not only removes the sinner from his sin but removes the sin from the sinner. Just as God closed the Red Sea to prevent Israel from returning to Egypt when she became discouraged with the wilderness, so God removes our confessed sins so far that they cannot be found. If we must have sins, we must create new ones, for the old ones have been transported beyond us.

Several generations later another king of Judah had occasion to speak of the limitless periphery of God's forgiveness. Hezekiah had been told by the prophet Isaiah that he was going to die. In deep supplication Hezekiah pleaded with the Lord for an extension of life and was granted an additional fifteen years. When he recovered he wrote down the essence of his prayer, his repentance, and his rejoicing, and in it he said, ". . . thou hast cast all my sins behind thy back" (Isaiah 38:17). Hezekiah envisioned God treating his sins as a worthless thing to be disinterestedly thrown behind His back. He couldn't conceive of God placing his sins in a filing cabinet or programming them into heaven's computer system; they were merely flung behind Him as a part of the past that would never be relived or rehashed again. They were out of view, "behind thy back"; they were out of hand, "thou hast cast"; and they were totally gone, "all my sins." As a boy flings a rock into a pond, God has cast our sins away from His presence.

Isaiah, who recorded these words of King Hezekiah, also recorded the words of the King of Kings when he quoted the Lord as saying, "I, even I, am he that blotteth out thy transgressions for mine own sake, and will not remember thy sins" (Isaiah 43:25); and "I have blotted out, as a thick cloud, thy transgressions, and, as a cloud, thy sins: return unto me; for I have redeemed thee" (Isaiah 44:22). Blotted out—obliterated from view—engulfed in the cloud of His presence; such is God's disposition of our sins. They are erased by Christ's blood and encased in the cloud of God's glory. To recover our sins we must remove God's glory, and there is no power on earth or in hell that can shift the cloud of God's glory even a fraction of an inch.

In speaking of the covenant God intended to make with His people, wherein He would put His law in man's heart rather than on tables of stone and would relate to the people as their God and they to Him as His people, the Lord told Jeremiah, ". . . I will forgive their iniquity, and I will remember their sin no more" (Jeremiah 31:34). "I will forgive and forget." What a beautiful combination. How can you place a limit on the boundaries of God's forgiveness when He declares He forgets every sin that we confess? Forgiveness of today's sin is not qualified by the number of previous sins we may have confessed in the past, for God has no memory of them. They are as nothing; they are forgotten.

But there is still a sixth Old Testament passage that shows just how completely God forgives the penitent one.

"Who is a God like unto thee, that pardoneth iniquity, and passeth by the transgression of the remnant of his heritage? he retaineth not his anger for ever, because he delighteth in mercy. He will turn again, he will have compassion upon us; he will subdue our iniquities; and *thou wilt cast all their sins into the depths of the sea*" (Micah 7:18, 19, emphasis added). New York City may have thought she was original when, years ago, she began to barge her garbage out into the ocean to dispose of it by burial at sea, but God has been doing that with man's sins ever since man started to repent. Some have called this "the Sea of God's Forgetfulness" and have suggested that He has erected a sign, "No Fishing Allowed." Whatever the name of the sea may be, I'm confident that it is sufficiently large enough to "deep-six" our sins forever.

But the Old Testament does not have an exclusive on expressions that reveal the unlimited periphery in forgiveness. The New Testament, through the richness of the original Greek, pictures this immeasurable boundary equally well.

Right from the very beginning we are told that Jesus "saves" us from sin (*see* Matthew 1:21). Lost as the sheep on the hillside, sinking as Peter beneath the waves, bound as a prisoner enroute to his Roman imprisonment, we have been rescued by Jesus at the cost of His own life. We have been "saved" from whatever sin was doing to us, and "from the wrath to come" (*see* 1 Thessalonians 1:10).

We have also seen that our sins have been "wiped out" (*see* Acts 3:19) just as a chalkboard is erased in order to write a new lesson on it. God's forgiveness erases, wipes out, and obliterates all evidence of our sins.

Similarly, the New Testament is fond of speaking of our being "washed from sin" (*see* Acts 22:16). It is as though God takes our stained, soiled, sticky lives and puts them in an automatic washer. His forgiveness is a powerful detergent that cleanses every stain. The record may be "wiped out," but our sins are "washed out." Forgiveness handles both the penalty and the pollution of sin.

Romans 4:7 says, ". . . Blessed are they whose iniquities are forgiven, and whose sins are covered." And the Greek verb used for "covered" is *epikaluptein,* which, in secular use, is used of snow obliterating a road and of someone blindfolding his eyes so that he cannot see. God has blanketed out, covered over, hidden our sins from not only His view but from the view of others.

Forgiveness and forgetting are inseparable with God. Hallelujah!

But the New Testament has more to say about this unlimited periphery in forgiveness. In the mercy of God our sins are not "reckoned" against us (*see* Romans 4:8 RSV). Reckoned is an accountant's term, which literally means "to set down to someone's account." When God forgives, He balances our account records. Our sins are no longer listed in the credit ledger; they are not seen as liabilities or accounts receivable; they have been "paid in full." Since Christ is for us, our sins cannot be reckoned against us!

Complementary to this, God's forgiveness "put away [our] sin" (*see* Hebrews 9:26). The Greek word used here, *athetesis,* is a technical, legal term used for the cancellation of a contract or an agreement. Whatever contractual arrangement we may have made with sin, Satan, or sinners, God's forgiveness cancels it. It is overridden by a higher law. Just as in the Old Testament a husband could overrule any vow his wife made (*see* Numbers 30:8), so at conversion our heavenly bridegroom overrules all contracts that are not in the best interest of our combined lives.

God's forgiveness has also made us "free from sin" (*see* Romans 6:18; 8:2). We are liberated and released from sin.

The word used here means "to give someone his freedom." We who had become slaves to sin have, by God's forgiveness, been emancipated, brought back, and set at liberty. When Jesus preached in the synagogue in His hometown He read: "The Spirit of the Lord God is upon me; because the Lord hath anointed me to . . . proclaim liberty to the captives, and the opening of the prison to them that are bound" (Isaiah 61:1). Forgiveness frees!

So whether we use the Old Testament pictures to see our sins as being sealed up in a bag, removed into infinity, cast behind His back, blotted out, remembered no more, and cast into the depths of the sea; or whether we view the New Testament concepts of forgiveness providing a Saviour, wiping out the record, washing the stain of sin, covering the marks of sin like a snowfall, settling the accounts, and cancelling our contracts; we should be comforted in knowing that God's forgiveness is limitless. It is never partial; it is always total. From God's point of view sin has been forgiven, forgotten, and flung away: from our perspective sin has been remitted, removed, and relegated to oblivion. How great is His mercy toward us, and so unlimited is His forgiveness.

Nevertheless, for this unlimited periphery of forgiveness to be effectual in our day-by-day experience, there must also be a continuous progression in forgiveness, for it can never be predated. I cannot repent today for sins that I may anticipate committing tomorrow, although I can, of course, repent of the desire to commit them.

Certainly we want to live above sin. God's Word assures us of this right. But we do well to realize that God does not expect instant perfection of behavior, even after we have earnestly repented of our sins and have been genuinely born again. Failures are expected. We may not act like saints as yet, for we are actually saints in the making, and the process allows for mistakes, errors, and sins.

John the beloved seemed to have a good grasp on this fact, for he wrote, "If we say that we have no sin, we deceive ourselves, and the truth is not in us. If we say that we have not sinned, we make him a liar, and his word is not in us" (1 John 1:8, 10). This epistle was written to Christians, not to sinners. It was penned to those who had already repented of sin and confessed Christ as Lord and Saviour, and yet to them he declares that taking a position of being sinless is to walk in self-deceit.

Matthew Henry reminds us, in his *New One Volume Edition Commentary on the Whole Bible:* "The Christian religion is the religion of sinners. The Christian life is a life of continued repentance, of continual faith in, thankfulness for, and love to the Redeemer." Day by day, as the Holy Spirit makes us aware of inward sin, we repent of it and receive fresh forgiveness. John balances his assertion that we are not above sin by saying, "If we confess our sins, he is faithful and just to forgive us our sins, and to cleanse us from all unrighteousness" (1 John 1:9) and, ". . . if any man sin, we have an advocate with the Father, Jesus Christ the righteous" (1 John 2:1). Although we do not come into perfection overnight, every sin that is uncovered in our life has a blood cleansing on the earth and an advocate with the Father in heaven. Forgiveness handles present sin as effectively as it handled past sin.

This concept of continuous progression in forgiveness is pointed out in John's assertion that ". . . if we walk in the light, as he is in the light, we have fellowship one with another, and the blood of Jesus Christ his Son cleanseth us from all sin" (1 John 1:7). *The New English Bible* translates that last phrase, "and we are being cleansed from every sin by the blood of Jesus . . . ." The walking in the light is progressive, step-by-step, and the cleansing is equally progressive, step-by-step.

As long as we will walk and talk with God, His forgiveness and cleansing flow continually. The greater the degree of light we walk in, the greater revelation of sin, and therefore the greater level of forgiveness that is afforded us.

So often we hear testimonies that date the person's forgiveness to some point in their past where they "got saved," but the forgiveness God offers to the believer cannot be so easily dated for it is updated regularly. I have been forgiven, I am being forgiven, and I shall be forgiven.

But when have I gone beyond promise and into presumption? How often may I expect God's forgiveness?

What did Jesus require of Peter? "Then came Peter to him, and said, Lord, how oft shall my brother sin against me, and I forgive him? till seven times? Jesus saith unto him, I say not unto thee, Until seven times: but, Until seventy times seven" (Matthew 18:21, 22). Peter was told that a true disciple should be willing and able to forgive a sinning brother at least four hundred ninety times a day. If my pocket calculator is to be trusted, that is once every 1.959 minutes in a sixteen-hour day. If man is required to forgive at least every two minutes of a long day, would God do any less? Of course not. As often as there is genuine repentance offered to God, there will be gracious forgiveness offered to man. Is not that the way of a parent with a child?

The first book that I ever wrote had a circulation of only one. I wrote it as a Christmas present for my youngest daughter, Tina. She was in her teen years and seemed to be in violation of one regulation of the home after another. I found myself in the role of judge far too often. Her Christmas book had only twelve pages and, aside from the month at the top of the page, each page read the same: "This page grants to Tina exemption from punishment for one misdeed during the above month if this page is presented to her father before judgment is meted out." My goal was to help her grasp more fully the forgiveness of her heavenly Father.

The book was one of her favorite gifts and was kept on the dresser in her bedroom. The first time she used it, she was fearful that it might be a joke, but the moment she walked into the house she was aware that I had found out something pretty severe. She ran to her bedroom, grabbed the book, and timidly came out to meet me, holding the book in front of her without saying a word. This caught me by surprise, and I stopped speaking in midsentence. I never picked up the discussion again; I merely took the book and removed the page of the month.

"Don't you want to talk about it?" she asked.

"I can't," I said, "for I have forgiven it."

I was proud of the lesson that I was teaching her, until the Lord asked me if I would like to be limited to one forgiveness per month. I realized then that I had only partially grasped and revealed the mercy and magnitude of God's forgiveness. I had put a limit on an unlimited provision.

How many of us are doing the same thing in our concepts of God's forgiveness? There is no limit; it is progressive and has a boundless periphery, but our little faith can scale down God's great gift until we have only a miniature representation instead of a monumental original.

And the glory of the "real thing," the true divine forgiveness, is that it is permanent, guaranteed forever—not as man views forever in the span of time—but as God sees it in His involvement with eternity. There is no end to the forgiveness of God, for it is eternal and everlasting. The psalmist recognized this when he wrote the one hundred thirty-sixth psalm, for every verse in this psalm ends with, ". . . for his mercy endureth forever." Repeatedly I have had congregations stand while I divided them into two groups and asked them to face each other. Then I had them read this psalm antiphonally, requesting that the people who repeated the words "for his mercy endureth forever" shout them out. Sometimes it got through to the people that God's mercy doesn't endure for "twiceth or thriceth" but forever.

Forgiveness, which is one manifestation of God's mercy, is forever. Hebrews speaks of our "eternal redemption" (9:12), our "eternal salvation" (5:9), and of God's "everlasting covenant" (13:20), and each time the word used is *aionios,* a word that is used over forty times in the New Testament in connection with "eternal life." This word is also applied to God's endless existence (*see* Romans 16:46) and is used in describing eternal punishment (*see* Matthew 25:46) and eternal judgment (*see* Mark 3:29). So God's forgiveness of our sins is as lasting as His existence, and His provision of forgiveness lingers as long as His term of punishment for those who will not repent and forsake their sins.

And how could we expect anything less? Since forgiving us is a manifestation of the essential nature of God and becomes a channel for God's glory to be manifested on the earth, surely it could not have a duration any shorter than its source. God always was, always is, and always shall be, and His forgiveness always was, always is, and always shall be. There is no possibility that He will change His decrees, for one of the concluding statements of the Old Testament is, "For I am the Lord, I change not; therefore ye sons of Jacob are not consumed" (Malachi 3:6). The New Testament says much the same thing: "Jesus Christ the same yesterday, and to day, and for ever" (Hebrews 13:8). Just as there is no yesterday in God's concepts, so there is no tomorrow. God deals in one great, eternal *now.* Our sins are forgiven throughout this immeasurable period of eternity that boggles the imagination of the human intellect.

In trying to help our time-bound minds to comprehend the expanse of eternity and the tremendous permanence of God's forgiveness, someone has suggested that if a bird would carry a single grain of sand in its beak and could fly to the moon, making the round trip every thousand years, by the time it had transported all of the sands of the seashores, and all of the grains of sand that make up the world's vast deserts, eternity would only have completed its first day of time. Just so, God has extended His forgiveness to encompass a span of time that matches our eternal existence with Him in heaven. We will never, ever, under any circumstances have to face our sin at any point in eternity, once it has been sincerely confessed here in time. Our judgment of sin does not await us; it is behind us. Only the judgment of our works lies ahead, and that is to determine the rewards we are to receive, not whether we are to be allowed entrance into God's heaven.

So let us enjoy forgiveness. David did! He used to sing, "Blessed is he whose transgression is forgiven, whose sin is covered. Blessed is the man unto whom the Lord imputeth not iniquity, and in whose spirit there is no guile" (Psalms 32:1, 2). Is our guilt equal to his guilt of adultery and murder? Yet he found such forgiveness that his song returned and he enjoyed genuine happiness.

Let us enjoy forgiveness. Paul did! This man, who was consenting unto Stephen's death and personally saw to the slaughter of countless martyrs, so rejoiced in God's complete and full forgiveness that he actually sang David's song (*see* Romans 4:7) even though he often had to sing it in some primitive jail. He was given to rejoicing and constantly urged others to "rejoice in the Lord" (Philippians 3:1).

Let us enjoy forgiveness. Peter did! After miserably denying his Lord, he followed Christ's footsteps in service to

God and wrote, "Simon Peter, a servant and an apostle of Jesus Christ," [that doesn't sound like he was living in guilt] "to them that have obtained *like* precious faith *with us* through the righteousness of God and our Saviour Jesus Christ" (2 Peter 1:1, emphasis added).

Let us enjoy forgiveness. We have been restored to a whole new life. Let's live it. Let's lock up the memories of our past sins and embrace the glories of a sinless present. Let's stop punishing ourselves trying to "help God out" and start enjoying our release from sin's penalty, pollution, power, and guilt. We have been justified; let's enjoy it. In Christ we have been sanctified; let's savor it to the fullest. We are being glorified; let's delight in it. Let's stop listening to our memory circuits and reprogram our minds to enjoy our new status as forgiven and loved people.

The handcuffs have been removed. Rejoice!

The contract has been cancelled. Sing!

The debt has been paid. Shout!

God's love has triumphed over His law. Enjoy it!

Let's enjoy forgiveness!